COMING OUT ALIVE!

Navigating Postmodern Philosophy and Culture

KAREN E. CEDERGREN

BARKER ☯ JULES

BARKER ❸ JULES®

COMING OUT ALIVE!

ISBN | : 978-1-64789-657-7
eBook ISBN | : 978-1-64789-658-4

BARKER & JULES, LLC
2248 Meridian Blvd. Ste. H, Minden, NV 89423
barkerandjules.com

Table of Contents

DEDICATION

To my parents and forever missionaries at heart, Revs. John (1929-2019) and Betty (1932-2019) Cedergren, who raised me right, instilling in me through the example of their own lives, a deep and abiding love for our Savior, Jesus Christ. They were coworkers with me in the ministry for over 30 years, my best friends, and dear to me beyond the expression of words or deeds.

To my mentor, the late Rev. Virgle J. Howell, affectionately known as "Bro. Howell." I owe so much of who I am today to his inspirational life and example and to the missions organization he founded, Rhema Christian Center, in Golden, MS, which has blessed me with friendship and legal covering since 1980.

To my Bible School alma mater, RHEMA Bible Training Center (College), in Tulsa, Oklahoma, and its founder, the late Rev. Kenneth E. Hagin, and RMAI. I am still living and ministering after the strong Word I received there and the high standards to which you held our generation.

To my "elder child," Rhema Christian Training Center in Tarlac City, Philippines, which proved to be a training ground for me, where the Holy Spirit sharpened my love for studying and teaching God's Word.

To the leadership and congregation of my "younger child," AGAPE Christian Centre, in Schlieren, Switzerland. I love you. Let's finish strong together!

Chapter Fourteen, entitled, "Trading Gold for Bronze – A Tale of Three Generations" is dedicated to Brian Solis who inspired its inclusion in this book.

Above all, to Jesus Christ be all the glory forever!

PREFACE

This is not a book on Sociology or Psychology. If you are expecting a super sophisticated, PhD level writing style herein, filled with long fifty-cent words, you will be disappointed.

If you should perceive anything written in this book as pushing a political position or feeding a political narrative, your perception is mistaken. This is not a political book.

The goal of this book is simply to bring awareness to the Church in general and each believer individually concerning the spirit of the age we are up against in an easy to read, easy to understand writing style and offer some Scriptural counsel as to how the disciple of Jesus Christ can successfully navigate through this mixed-up world we live in.

It is important for the reader to understand that the examples from my lifetime of experience and the stories used to illustrate a point about modern-day church practices are not the main point in, of and by themselves. Rather, they are used only as windows to let light shine in on the core issues raised.[1] It is my earnest prayer that the reader will not get caught up on the illustration and miss the point beneath it.

---

[1] Ephesians 5:13

None of the views in this book are intended to come across as judgmental, sarcastic or cynical. Each observation made and every question asked are made and asked with sobering sincerity.

My effort throughout this book will be aimed at offering Scriptural guidance so that the believer may be insulated from the infection of Postmodern philosophy and culture without being isolated from it.[2]

One of the three main verses of Scripture I have relied on for guidance in life and ministry is 2 Corinthians 2:1-5,

> *1 And when I came to you, brethren, I did not come with superiority of speech or of wisdom, proclaiming to you the testimony of God. 2 For I determined to know nothing among you except Jesus Christ, and Him crucified. 3 I was with you in weakness and in fear and in much trembling, 4 and my message and my preaching were not in persuasive words of wisdom, but in demonstration of the Spirit and of power, 5 so that your faith would not rest on the wisdom of men, but on the power of God.*

Throughout the pages of this book, it will be my earnest endeavor to remain faithful to the standard and expectation found in these verses.

I challenge the reader to actually doublecheck me on the more than 270 verses used or footnoted herein. Open your Bible and read them for yourself. You will be doubly blessed!

---

[2] John 17:15-17

INTRODUCTION

The Loveless Church - Ephesus [3]
2:7 "He who has an ear, let him hear what the Spirit says to the churches. To him who overcomes I will give to eat from the tree of life, which is in the midst of the Paradise of God."

The Persecuted Church - Smyrna
2:11 "He who has an ear, let him hear what the Spirit says to the churches. He who overcomes shall not be hurt by the second death."

The Compromising Church - Pergamos
2:17 "He who has an ear, let him hear what the Spirit says to the churches. To him who overcomes I will give some of the hidden manna to eat. And I will give him a white stone, and on the stone a new name written which no one knows except him who receives it."

---

[3] All verses here are from the NKJV, including the title descriptions for each verse.

The Corrupt Church - Thyatira

2:26 "And he who overcomes, and keeps My works until the end, to him I will give power over the nations— 27 'He shall rule them with a rod of iron; They shall be dashed to pieces like the potter's vessels'— as I also have received from My Father; 28 and I will give him the morning star. 29 "He who has an ear, let him hear what the Spirit says to the churches."

The Dead Church - Sardis

3:5 "He who overcomes shall be clothed in white garments, and I will not blot out his name from the Book of Life; but I will confess his name before My Father and before His angels. 6 He who has an ear, let him hear what the Spirit says to the churches."

The Faithful Church - Philadelphia

3:12 "He who overcomes, I will make him a pillar in the temple of My God, and he shall go out no more. I will write on him the name of My God and the name of the city of My God, the New Jerusalem, which comes down out of heaven from My God. And I will write on him My new name. 13 He who has an ear, let him hear what the Spirit says to the churches."

The Lukewarm Church - Laodicea

3:21 "To him who overcomes I will grant to sit with Me on My throne, as I also overcame and sat down with My Father on His throne. 22 He who has an ear, let him hear what the Spirit says to the churches."

I am beginning this book by sharing these inspiring promises from Revelation chapters two and three to assure the reader that the ultimate goal of the message herein is one of equipping, hope and final victory for the born-again child of God, not judgmental criticism, gloom and doom, or pessimism and defeat.

Having said that, it is nevertheless not a very popular thing in the atmosphere of this generation to confront or rub against modern-day culture. It is not popular or easy for the Christian to stand up to contemporary culture. More alarming, however, is the fact that it is also becoming taboo within the family of Christian faith to challenge or question the standards, methods and practices which have become mainstream in much of Christianity and church ministry in this Postmodern environment.

This message has been growing inside me for quite some time... maybe as long as twenty years now and it almost feels like it is already about a half dozen years too late in its release!

What finally pushed me over the edge, so-to-speak, in taking the book-writing plunge, was the first comment to a poll question I posted in a private social media chat group in 2017. Based on the very first comment, I knew right away that what this generation of professed believers in Jesus Christ needed is stronger, more Biblically sound teaching rather than more space for the airing of Postmodern views and philosophies that have infiltrated their culture and theology.

The hypothetical question I posed to the pastors in the private social media chat group went something like this:

"To you pastors, how would you handle the following scenario: Your nephew is in his twenties and about to get married. He was born in a Hindu country but adopted as a baby and grew up in a modern, secular, western country, culture, and society. His adoptive family raised him in nominal denominational Christianity. As he grew into adulthood, however, he gravitated ever more towards the culture and customs of the

Hindu nation in which he was born but never knew. He is your relative and has asked you to co-officiate their wedding. He explains to you that he is also planning to incorporate some 'aspects' from the culture of the country of his birth into the wedding ceremony which will be handled by his friend who is from the same Hindu country. Being a Christian minister, you know how attached that country's culture is with the religion, Hinduism, so you ask for clarification as to what 'aspects' from that culture he plans to include. His answer alarms you because the 'aspects' he will include are rituals which are inextricably rooted in and linked to the worship of Hindu gods, although he assures you that he will only be using them from a cultural point-of-view, making no mention of the Hindu gods to which they pay homage. Because he is your relative and you love him, the pressure and expectation are compounded. Would you agree to co-officiate this wedding ceremony under these conditions?"

I wanted to get a sense as to how influenced the pastors in this private chat group have been by Postmodern philosophy and progressive theology. How far had they drifted away from the Gospel and Word training they had received while in the Bible School my parents and I founded in the Philippines in 1983?

Before any pastor had time to respond, a non-pastor graduate commented immediately that, in her opinion, it is not ours to judge the young man in the question but that we should just accept, respect, and comply with his wishes… That since it is his wedding the young man has the right to incorporate anything into his wedding he wants, and no one has the right to attempt to counsel him that it is not appropriate to mix these Hindu-laced rituals into a "Christian" wedding ceremony. Just respect and give way to his wishes was the sentiment of the commenter.

There it was on full display in one split-second of time: full-blown Postmodern philosophy shining brightly through this young believer's comment.

Right then, I realized that by posing the poll question and seeking for pastors' responses, I had become an unintentional enabler for the propagation of Postmodern philosophy. That was it! The post came down and the Holy Spirit began to impress upon me the need to write this book.

Certainly, the young groom-to-be and his fiancé are entitled to include anything they want in their wedding ceremony, but the larger question was whether or not the pastors in the chat group would have agreed to co-officiate a wedding that would include Hindu-laced customs and rituals side-by-side with Christian wedding elements and Bible verses. As little as a decade ago, I believe the answer from the majority of these Bible School trained pastors would have been a resounding, "No!"

But how about now? How far had these Evangelical and Pentecostal ministers drifted from the roots of Biblical Christianity, migrating into their theology the newest, coolest elements of progressive theology in order to fit in, cater to and patronize the Postmodern culture around them?

If your answer to the hypothetical question posed above is the same as that of the young commenter in the chat group, then you especially need the message in this book! Your Christianity and worldview have been infiltrated and shaped by Postmodernism. You are Postmodern for sure, and quite likely, also a Millennial or Generation Z-er. The question as to what that all means and why succumbing to Postmodernism by embracing it is dangerous to your Christian faith will be answered in the pages of this book.

Unfortunately, most polls and research studies in the totality of topics discussed in this book are based on the U.S. population and society. There are not an abundance of polls and research studies for the rest of the world on these issues. Nevertheless, I believe it is reasonable to use U.S. based studies in the search for understanding the effects of Modernism and Postmodernism in our world. Two little catchphrases underline the impact of "Americanism" on the rest of the world.

The first catchphrase is one I remember hearing when I lived in the Philippines in the 1980s, "When America sneezes, the Philippines catches a cold."

The second catchphrase that one can often hear outside the U.S. is, "As America goes, so goes the rest of the world."

These catchphrases describe the strong influence that American culture and economy have on the rest of the world. This explains why so many of the footnotes in this book note U.S. statics, resources, and quotes.

As far as writing style goes, I will unapologetically buck the headwinds of political correctness and Postmodern norms by freely using the terms "he," "his," "man", "men," and "mankind" when referring to the entire human race or generic qualities and issues which are found in both men and women. I will not stop in each instance to re-qualify their context or meaning. However, for the readers of this generation who have grown up under Modern and Postmodern cultures, women's lib indoctrination, and have grown accustomed to using degenderizing terms (i.e.: "post-person" instead of postman, "policeperson" instead of policeman, "humankind" instead of mankind, etc.) which are now mainstream in society because they are considered more politically correct, I will offer the following help point:

I will always italicize the words *"he," "his," "him," "man," "men,"* and *"mankind"* when referring to the whole human race or any quality common to both genders as we work together to unravel the reader's Modern-Postmodern indoctrination in this area of political correctness.

Genesis 5:2 says,

He created them male and female, and He blessed them and named them man in the day when they were created. [4]

The Bible says, when God created man, He created them male and female, blessed them both and called them both *"man."* You see, heaven operates by a completely different and opposite set of thought patterns and values than *man* does here on earth.

We will learn in this book that terms such as, *"he," "him," "man,"* and *"mankind,"* when referring to the whole of humanity or discussing traits common to both genders, are not sexist, chauvinist or misogynist.

Lady readers, there is no need to go ballistic over their use... for this author is also female.

---

[4] (emphasis added) Rendered "man" in the following major Bible translations: TLB, ESV, NASB1977, NASB, HCSB, JB2000 and Young's Translation. The Amplified and NIV use the word "mankind". Rendered "Adam" in the following translations: KJV, NHEB, KJ2000, AKJV, ASV, Douay-Rheims, Darby, ERV, OJB, Webster's Bible and WEB. Of the major translations and paraphrases, only the following cave to politically correct verbiage: NLT, ISV, God's Word and NET Bible.

Coming Out Alive!

Chapter One

PREMODERNISM

> *Thus says the LORD, the King of Israel*
> *And his Redeemer, the LORD of hosts:*
> *'I am the first and I am the last,*
> *And there is no God besides Me.'*
> *Isaiah 44:6*

Understanding our world today requires an understanding of how we got to this point in time.

Before we can begin to understand the impact of Postmodernism on society in general, on the Church specifically -- and more importantly, how to counter its impact in the believer's life -- we need a basic framework of definitions and historical overview from which to work.

To date, sociologists have divided the human story into three broad philosophical eras or epochs. Each epoch received its designation based on several factors in play in the development of humanity at that point in time, such as arts, science, literature, culture, religion, philosophy, etc. The sum total of these contributing factors form a fundamental "worldview" which drives society and the human mindset at that point in time.

The transition dates from one socio-philosophical epoch to the next can vary tremendously. I have examined several variations and decided to use dates that "make sense" in my purview but let us not stumble over whether we agree or disagree on the issue of which dates are used here as the framework for our study because the dates of these eras are not primary point of this book. Epochs, eras, movements and dispensations never start and stop in a nice, neat, cut and dry fashion. There are always huge swaths of overlap to every transition… hence, the great diversity in the dating system. This is the way it is when dating history and historical events. Some dates are solid. Still, for much of world history, the date variations and transition times can differ by just a few years. Other times they can run into hundreds of years.

The Premodern Era – The Philosophy of Theism

Time Span: from Genesis 1:1 to roughly the middle of the nineteenth century (i.e.: the 1800s), although some sociologists would contend that the Premodern Era was in slow decline and transition beginning in the middle seventeenth century. Our time span for the Premodern Era covers a broad span of approximately 5,500-5,800 years.

Premodernism is defined by the following characteristics:

• Belief in the supernatural (the Judeo-Christian God of the Bible or, in the case of the rest of humanity, "gods").

• Truth is fixed, inviolable, absolute and can be known or discovered. Discovery of it is only available by going to its source which is the supernatural. For the Jew and Christian, that meant that the source for the discovery of this fixed and absolute Truth is the God of the Bible. For everyone else, false gods and myths were developed, sought out and relied upon in attempting to explain the unexplainable.

• *Man* is accountable for this Truth (i.e.: to search out and find it). It is *his* inherent goal and responsibility to search for this fixed and absolute Truth and *his* authority in life comes from God (i.e.: the supernatural).

- The universe is ordered.
- The supernatural is at the center of the universe.
- Knowledge starts with God (i.e.: the supernatural).
- Conviction is a virtue.
- Tolerance that compromises on matters of conviction is evil.
- Defining and pursuing purpose is above all.
- Clear sense of identity.
- Personal independence, responsibility, and privacy are to be pursued, cherished, and guarded.
- Change in *man's* behavior comes about by adhering to the standard based on that fixed and absolute Truth... as much as is possible considering *man's* fallibility.
- Theologically, in the Premodern worldview, belief in God (theism) or in the case of pagans, "gods" (animism, polytheism and pantheism) were at the center of the universe.

Premodernism is not the reason behind Biblical Christianity nor is it the explanation for the belief in the Judeo-Christian God of the Bible, to be sure. Believing that would play right into Modern and Postmodern biases. Instead, it is the other way around.

Everything begins with God.

The one True, Living and Everlasting God Who is, Who was, and Who is to come. He is infinite past and future and chose to reveal Himself to *mankind* through creation, through His Word, the Bible, and ultimately through the advent of His Son, Jesus Christ of Nazareth.[5] Without this Self-revelation, *man* would never, could never know anything about God, *himself,* life, morality or anything else. Everything begins with God. He is the Originator of all things visible and invisible.

---

[5] Romans 1:20; John 1:1-14; Hebrews 1:1-4; I Corinthians 2:6-10; 2 Timothy 3:16

Here are a few verses which bring this truth to light:

In the beginning, God... [6]

Before the mountains were born or You gave birth to the earth and the world, Even from everlasting to everlasting, You are God. [7]

Even from eternity I am He... [8]

And the Word became flesh, and dwelt among us; and we saw His glory, glory as of the only Son from the Father, full of grace and truth. [9]

Now to the King eternal, immortal, invisible, the only God, be honor and glory forever and ever. Amen. [10]

...He who is the blessed and only Sovereign, the King of kings and Lord of lords, who alone possesses immortality and dwells in unapproachable light, whom no man has seen or can see. To Him be honor and eternal dominion! Amen [11]

Everything begins with God.

It isn't Premodernism that gave "God" to Judaism and Christianity. God is not the product or result of Premodernism.

---

[6] Genesis 1:1
[7] Psalm 90:2
[8] Isaiah 43:13
[9] John 1:14
[10] I Timothy 1:17
[11] I Timothy 6:15-16

Creation itself would not exist if there was not God first! The Bible tells us that all things have come into being by Him and that nothing that exists came into being without Him.[12]

God didn't need Premodernism. He simply chose to reveal and share Himself with His creation… And for 5,500-6,000 years, *man* accepted the truth that God (i.e.: the supernatural) exists.

Christians today need not to be labeled as "premodernists," "old-fashioned," or "backwards" because they believe in the Judeo-Christian God of the Bible, because the God we believe in existed long before He created the world and He will continue to exist even after Modernism, Postmodernism, or any future epochs, yet-unnamed, are long gone! God is greater than time, greater than epochs, greater than everything seen and unseen! [13]

Biblical Christianity transcends every sociological and philosophical era labeled by *man*, including Premodernism.

Premodernism. Modernism. Postmodernism. What are they but labels of time established by men?

Here is the greater truth:

The light, life and love of God pierces every open heart in every epoch of time! The ready heart will believe in Him regardless the sociological, philosophical era!

As the saying goes, "Wise *men* still seek Him."

---

[12] John 1:3

[13] Revelation 1:8, 17-18; 21:6; 22:13

CHAPTER TWO

MODERNISM

> ❝
>
> *The fool says in his heart, 'There is no God.'*
> *Psalm 14:1*

The Modern Era – The Philosophy of Denial

Time Span: from roughly the middle of the 19th century (the 1800s) up to the middle – late 20th century (roughly the 1980s). Note: some sociologists and historians place the very beginnings of the Modern Era as early as the middle 1600s, but I'm going to stick with the time frame given above.

Notice how dramatically the life span of this era shrunk compared to the Premodern Era. This era covers a time period of around just 100-150 years conservatively speaking to maybe two to three hundred years if generosity is applied to the dating procedure.

For the better part of 5,000 years, *man* took as a given, the existence of the supernatural, unseen realm, but with the transition to the Modern

Era, in the relatively short span of just 100-300 years, some 5,000-6,000 years of Premodern norms were upended.

The Modern Era did not rule long but its impact was truly devastating as illustrated in the following redo of a 1922 cartoon by E.J. Pace.[14]

Characteristics of the Modern Age:

• Anti-supernatural. The supernatural does not exist. Rejects the idea of a compassionate, all-powerful Creator.

• There is no fixed, inviable, absolute truth to be known or discovered. There is no truth and no higher power to which *man* is accountable.

• Science, human reason, logic and rational are the only absolutes that exist. Revelation and *man's* dependence thereof is rejected.

• The **theory** of evolution is introduced by agnostic, Charles Darwin, in 1858 as the explanation for *man's* existence and becomes essential to Modern philosophy.

---

[14] Above graphic by Setsuri Solis ©2021. All rights reserved. It is a remake of a Christian cartoon by E.J. Pace; researchgate.net/figure/Cartoon-illustrating-the-Descent-of-the-Modernists-E-J-Pace-Christian-Cartoons-1922_fig2_350356802

• There is gradual movement in society away from agrarianism and towards industrialism, materialism, secularism, and rationalism.

• The authority which governs *mankind's* behavior is derived from logic and science. Only what can be proven scientifically is "true."

• Change is brought about by *man's* self-empowerment based only on what is logical and rational.

• "Modernism was essentially based on a utopian vision of human life and society and a belief in progress or moving forward."[15]

• Theologically, deistic agnosticism and atheism filled the Modernistic philosophy and worldview. *Man* becomes the center of the universe under Modernism.

Modernism is the diametrical opposite of Premodernism. It used the proverbial "bull in the china shop" approach as it was taking over and pushing out the Premodern Era. It spared nothing from the Premodern Era. Took no hostages, no prisoners and brought with it into the new era no souvenirs. Everything "Premodern" was to be rejected and utterly repudiated.

At the core of the Modern philosophy is nihilism, which is defined as,

the rejection of all religious and moral principles, in the belief that life is meaningless.[16]

Modernism focuses heavily on materialism and hedonism. What else is there if you deny the existence of a life after this one? Modernism has nothing to offer for the life that follows after this one because it doesn't believe there is one. When you die, it's all over. You are just dead like a dog.

---

[15] courses.lumenlearning.com/boundless-arthistory/chapter/the-rise-of-modernism/

[16] lexico.com/definition/nihilism

Biblical Christianity, on the other hand, offers the promise and expectant hope of heaven and eternal life through faith in Jesus Christ.[17]

Side Note

The terms "modernization" and "modernism" are mutually exclusive and should not be mistakenly interchanged as synonyms.

Modernization is the act of making something more modern,[18] whereas, Modernism is a philosophical worldview and a philosophical era in the sociological history of *man*.

For the most part, modernization is a blessing to our lives. Like money, modernization is neither moral nor immoral. It is neutral. In the hands of good people, many great things that help all of humanity are possible because of it, but in the hands of people with darkened hearts, modernization can be used in some very greedy and evil ways.

Always remember:

Modernization is simply amoral, but Modernism is just plain immoral.

---

[17] John 3:16; John 14:1-4; 1 Peter 3:15; 1 Corinthians 15:1-58
[18] dictionary.cambridge.org/dictionary/english/modernization

CHAPTER THREE

POSTMODERNISM

> *In those days there was no king in Israel;*
> *everyone did what was right in his own eyes.*
> *Judges 21:25*

The Postmodern Era –The Philosophy of No Absolutes

Time Span: from roughly the 1980s to the present day (although some experts assign 1945 – or the end of World War II – as the starting point for the Postmodern Age). We are just about 50 years into the Postmodern Age at the time of this writing. Maybe seventy some odd years at most.[19]

PREMODERN	MODERN	POSTMODERN
•	↗	(scribble)
" Because God put it there, period. "	" Man makes his own inevitable progress. "	" qwefbln@# jsidh$%ka th&alk*+! "

---

[19] Graphic art by Setsuri Solis ©2021; All rights reserved.

The Characteristics that Define Postmodernism are:

• God, truth, and absolutes might exist… or they might not, no one can say for sure.

• No one has the right to say that their belief is the truth. There is no ultimate authority to guide *man*.

• Everyone's belief about God, truth, and absolutes are a matter of their own personal interpretation and opinion.

• In the Postmodern world, nothing can be known for certain. It is the world of "I'm okay, you're okay" and, "If it feels good, do it."

• Reality and truth are whatever the individual wants them to be. The keyword for everything is: *"whatever…"*

• Everything in the worldview of the Postmodernist is a matter of one's own interpretation and, each person's interpretation is as good as the other's.

• Change is contingent on self-expression and culture.

• Tolerance, acceptance of, and subjection to, the Postmodern lifestyle and culture is demanded of others, yet for the most part, tolerance is not afforded to those who hold a point of view which is contrary to or considered out-of-sync with their own.

• Theologically, where Modern Era philosophy outright denied the existence of the supernatural realm, the Postmodernist believes the supernatural might exist… but, once again in their worldview, no one can know for sure. This sets up the Postmodernist very well for assimilating some supernatural beliefs into their lifestyle. For example, it would not be contradictory or unusual for a Postmodern person to engage in paranormal activities, such as embracing elements of New Age, Wicca, Hindu, or Buddhist beliefs and philosophies into their worldview and daily lives. It is not needful for the Postmodernist to fully reject the supernatural as the Modernist does. Only Biblical Christianity is offensive.

- In the mind of the Postmodernist, Biblical Christianity is *mankind's* biggest enemy. As the whole world is swallowed up by Postmodernism, Post-Christian society follows right behind. Postmodernism equals Post-Christian.

Postmodernism Exemplified in the Book of Judges

In the days of the Book of Judges, Israel had no king, and everyone did their own thing.[20] That anarchy resulted in the nation being subjugated under various oppressors at least seven times for a total of around 111 of the 400 years of Jewish history covered in the book. Truth told, even one year... no, even one day is too long to be out of fellowship with God.

But how did the nation go so quickly from the conquest victories recounted throughout the preceding Book of Joshua to a vicious 400 year cycle of Sin, Servitude, Sorrow, Salvation? Judges 2:10 gives us the answer:

> *10 And all that (Joshua) generation also were gathered to their fathers; and there arose another generation after them who did not know the Lord, nor yet the work which He had done for Israel. (parenthesis added)*

Somehow, the generation under Joshua failed to successfully pass on to the succeeding generation a healthy respect for and trust in the God who had delivered them from Egypt and the wilderness, and planted them in the land promised to their fathers, Abraham, Isaac, and Jacob.

The generation of Israelites in the Book of Judges was an Emergent generation. You will learn what that means later in this book. They had devolved into a congregation which discarded the faith of their forefathers. Without that foundation, they had no training in the exercise of their faith and no moral scruples! And, they paid the price for it.

---

[20] Judges 17:6; 21:25

When a person, church, society or nation fails to give God the place He rightfully deserves, the result is chaos and anarchy.[21] This is what Postmodernism produces in the soul of *man*, church, society, and nation: chaos and anarchy.

Here is what the Postmodernist thinks about the Bible and anyone who is backward enough, in their eyes, to still believe in God:

> **Anyone who rejects evolution and favors old bibles from 2000 years ago, is a Premodernist. The Bible is premodern, outdated... A premodernist is an extreme conservative who still holds on to old fairy tale belief systems that have been proven wrong... Premodernism is cray cray!** [22]

Cray is urban slang for "crazy, silly, insane, stupid."

So that's it! If you believe in the Judeo-Christian God of the Bible today, you are "cray, cray" according to the Postmodernist.

The problem with their line of reasoning goes back to an important point we have already made:

Premodernism is not the source of the belief in the existence of God. God came first, period.

I didn't realize at the time, but I understand now, that the seeds of Postmodernism were germinating as far back as 1979-80, the year I spent in a Lutheran Liberal Arts College. But allow me to set up the backstory for you from a year earlier, to the year 1978.

1978 was the year the Lutheran Church in America released what came to be referred to by the LCA faithful as "the green hymnal." The green hymnal replaced the famous 1948 red hymnal. As a young, 17-year-old born-again Christian who had grown up in the Lutheran Church with

---

[21] Judges 2:20-23; Psalm 2:10-11, 33:12; Proverbs 11:14, 29:2

[22] wiki.c2.com/?PreModernism

the red hymnal, I was upset by the many changes that came with the new green covered hymnal. Even that many years ago, the editors of the new green hymnal had begun the descent into Postmodernism, political correctness, and liberal theology. Among the many step-down changes they made included replacing all gender specific lyrics, such as *"man"* or *"men"* (obviously referring to all *mankind*), in the hymns to gender neutral terms such as "they" and "them" and "friends." I have composed dozens of songs in my lifetime, the lyrics of which I certainly would not want tampered with 100 years from now!

I felt indignant, "Those editors do not have the right to change the lyrics of someone else's compositions!"

But what really irked me was the move from gender specific lyrics to gender neutral lyrics. I can remember fuming during our church's Christmas Eve Candlelight Service as we opened that fiendish green hymnal and began singing,

"Good Christian *friends* rejoice…" because I knew better!

The original lyrics to this 14th century Germanic-Latin Christmas hymn, translated into English in 1818,[23] actually went like this:

"Good Christian *men* rejoice…"

Those were the words that I had grown up singing and I saw no need for anyone to change them. Still don't!

So now, fast forward again to the following year, 1979, as I sat as a college freshman in my Basic Theology 101 class at Texas Lutheran College. Our professor wasted no time in introducing our class of 50-60 freshmen to liberal theology.

One day, he asked the class, "What do you think of our new green hymnal?"

I was the only one who raised their hand and answered, "I don't like it."

---

[23] hymnary.org (emphasis added)

The professor was taken back with my answer because most 18- and 19-year-old kids starting their college life couldn't care less what was going on in their LCA synod and home church! Red hymnal. Green hymnal. Is there a difference? Who cares?

Surprised that I even knew what he was talking about, he asked me why I did not like the new green hymnal. I explained to him that there was no need for the editors to change the lyrics in the hymns written by other people to gender neutral terminology. I told him that the word "man" meant all *mankind* in such contexts and need not be taken offensively by women. Then I said that if they removed the gender specific language in the hymns, perhaps the next hymnal the Lutheran Church put out would take this liberal theology junk a step even further and make all references to God gender neutral too!

The professor shot back, "Well, what would be the problem with that, since one-third of the Trinity is already an "it" (referring to the Holy Spirit)?"

Oh my! The professor of Basic Theology 101 in this supposedly Christian Liberal Arts college just called the Holy Spirit an "it!" I was flabbergasted! He did not know that the Bible teaches to us that the Holy Spirit is a Person with a personality and not an impersonal forcefield, not a cloud of cosmic energy, and certainly not an "it!" I was not yet so skilled in the Word so as to give a Scriptural rebuttal to prove him wrong, but I did know on the inside, in my spirit, that what he had just taught our class was, oh, so very wrong!

The seeds of Postmodernism were already germinating in 1979, and yet at that time, I had no understanding of the fact that the Premodern world was on the way out. I was already living in the declining days of the Modern Era. The subtle transition into Postmodernism had already begun!

2 Timothy 3:1-5 sums up perfectly this Postmodern Era:

1 But realize this, that in the last days difficult times will come. 2 For men will be lovers of self, lovers of money, boastful, arrogant, revilers, disobedient to parents, ungrateful, unholy, 3 unloving, irreconcilable, malicious gossips, without self-control, brutal, haters of good, 4 treacherous, reckless, conceited, lovers of pleasure rather than lovers of God, 5 holding to a form of godliness, although they have denied its power; Avoid such men as these.

Postmodernism is the Book of Judges playing out all over again in our time.

Chapter Four

POSTMODERN LIFE AND CULTURE

> *Anything I wanted, I would take. I denied myself no pleasure. I even found great pleasure in hard work, a reward for all my labors. 11 But as I looked at everything I had worked so hard to accomplish, it was all so meaningless—like chasing the wind. There was nothing really worthwhile anywhere.*
>
> *Ecclesiastes 2:10-11 (TLB)*

So, what is life under Postmodernism like? Are we able to recognize the time in which we are living?

Loss of Personal Privacy

The September 11th, 2001, attack in New York City was a pivotal moment in history, a watershed event. Its significance cannot be overstated. For everyone who was alive and old enough to remember that day, life changed almost instantly. Life changed permanently. We often mark modern time, memory, and history now by such terms as "before" and "after" 9-11.

Everything changed…. forever.

Travel and travel security began to change from that day on. As a result, governments have conditioned us to give up much of our personal privacy in the name of travel safety, national security and catching the bad guys.

Are you old enough to remember life before September 11, 2001? I am.

I have been a missionary my entire adult life, more than 40 years at the time of this writing, and I can remember what travel was like before 9-11.

Back in the "olden days" you could walk right up to the departure gate area in the airport when saying goodbye to your loved ones. The official luggage allowance for international flights "before 9-11" was a generous two free checked bags, each of which could weigh 70lbs (or 32 kilos). I made many trips to the Philippines back then, checking in with two heavy pressed-wood trunks each weighing nearly 100lbs and no one thought a thing about it! I was never charged for overweight bags. There was often no baggage security or screening. I can remember climbing onto airplanes with four or five heavy carry-ons slung around my neck, in addition to the two overweight 100lb trunks that were in checked baggage. There was no prescreening security checkpoint you had to clear before proceeding to your gate. You could carry your liquids right through. There was no need for you to remove your shoes and pass them through a scanner. No body scanners. Often no carry-on baggage scanners. Nothing… But not anymore! Not after 9-11. In order for us to travel safely today, we are conditioned to accept the loss of our privacy (and sometimes our dignity), all in the name of security.

I can understand the need for changes to the security systems governing travel because of dangers today, which basically did not exist pre-9-11, but it is the knock-on effects that should be troubling to all of us.

The Social Media Phenomenon

Travel safety *required* us to get used to giving up more of our privacy, but then, riding the coattails of 9-11, along came smartphones, GPS and social media, which prompted us to *voluntarily* expose even more of our private lives to the whole world via the world wide web.

In the early generations of social media sites, people mostly used aliases because they were still in the practice of protecting their privacy and personal data… but with the launch of Facebook in 2004, Postmodern *man* took the next step of voluntarily giving up personal privacy. It still astounds me that people are eager to report and chronicle almost every detail of their daily lives through pictures, posts, and "check-ins" on their social media timeline! Personal privacy is no longer held as something precious, something sacred, and something to be protected.

"Now, I'm at the bus stop… Checking in at Bus Stop H."

"Riding the bus, going to the dentist."

"Checking in at the Dentist."

"In the dentist chair."

"This is a selfie of my mouth open while the dentist is drilling out a cavity in my back molar."

"Finished with the dentist and on my way to eat lunch."

"Checking in at So-and-So Restaurant."

"Food photo of the big piece of sugar-filled, teeth-corrupting cheesecake I'm now eating."

On and on and on it goes…

Millennials, Gen X-ers, yes, and Baby Boomers too. Sorry, but I've got to tell it to you straight:

We really don't need the blow-by-blow chronicle of your day… every day! Nor do we really want to look at photos of your teeth!

How much have we grown accustomed to sharing nearly every thought, every emotion, and every detail of our location and activities on social media?

In the early days of social media, the earliest platforms like "MySpace" existed as forums for teenagers to hang out the dirty laundry of their bad behavior away from the prying eyes of their parents as they disguised and hid themselves through alias accounts.

The Gen X-ers were the target of the earliest social media platforms. In fact, the most famous social media platform today, Facebook, started out simply to offer college students a way to connect. One had to be enrolled in a college or university to gain access to it in its inception. It didn't take long, however, for the developers of Facebook to realize how willing people actually were to voluntarily "expose all" about their personal information, lives, whereabouts, thoughts, and activities. The founders of Facebook realized they had developed a bank-busting gold mine business by simply offering people a place to shed their privacy! Incredible!

From then on, it didn't take too long until the Baby Boomers and other generations discovered and "got the hang of" the most widely used social media platform in the world, claiming more than 2.85 billion users worldwide as of 2021. Think about it, approximately one out of every six humans walking this earth are users of that platform (or roughly 36% of the world's population). Just think about the intrusion into and power over our lives that we have handed over to these social media, big tech companies!

Today, though, Facebook is fast becoming thought of as the "old fashioned" platform for Baby Boomers and Gen X-ers. Younger generations, such as Millennials and Gen Z-ers, have already begun migrating to even newer social media platforms in order to get away from their meddlesome, middle-aged parents who are addicted to the older platform. How ironic that the platform which started out by targeting college-aged young people, Facebook, is now fast becoming the social platform site for "the older generation" as those now under 30 flee to newer social media formats such as, WhatsApp, Instagram, and TikTok.

Social media is a breeding ground for envy, jealousy, conflict, competition, and vanity. These run rampant in social media.

Christian believer, are you aware of the effects social media is having on your life? Studies have shown social media to be a major player in the break-up of marriages and friendships. Social media can be the perfect mask that many emotionally unhealthy people hide behind.

How many people project the image that their lives are sailing along beautifully through their photos and postings, only for the behind-the-scenes reality to be the complete opposite?

How did the emotional state of *man* come to a place of such degradation so as to desperately need and seek for affirmation from total strangers online?

Do you find yourself feeling sad, envious, angry, rejected, a failure, or even depressed by something you have seen on someone else's social media account?

How ridiculous is it that people do their fighting now before the whole world through their posts and comments? Even famous people, government officials, and politicians do this. International policies and negotiations are traded over social media today.

Trolling used to be a fishing word but in our Postmodern culture, it now refers to how one person intentionally tries to harass or incite another person to anger in social media. It also refers to the spying on other people's accounts that we engage in.

Young women, especially, can become addicted to posting photos, even provocative ones, in the vain search for the most "Likes" and "You are so beautiful" comments. This can lead to all kinds of private insecurities and wounds in the heart that all the virtual friends in the world cannot see.

Let us consider well how we use social media, dear reader. It would be worthwhile for us to train ourselves to resist the urging to post everything we do in order to boast or impress. The Bible says in 1 John 2:16 that boasting is the sin of the pride of life.

Your value and relevance as a person are not dependent upon receiving the affirmation of the whole world. Your value is set in the heart of God, not the bowels of social media.[24]

To have two genuine flesh and blood friends who see you as you really are and love you just the same, who help to hold you accountable in love,[25] is incomparably more valuable than having the affirmation of 10,000 virtual friends who do not know the true brokenness you may be experiencing on the inside.[26]

And Smartphones Galore!

And, how about our smartphones? What a blessing they are, right? Although technically speaking, cellular phones have been around since 1973, it wasn't until well into the 1990s that they started becoming a part of everyday life. In 2007, everything changed with Apple's first-generation iPhone.

We carry around more computer memory in our pocket today than what landed man on the moon in 1969!

Think about what our internet connected smartphones have replaced our need for: maps and GPS navigation devices, real books, hard copy tickets of all sorts, landline telephones, public phone booths (payphones), telephone books, address books, business cards, scanners, digital cameras, photo albums, camcorders, hard-wired home security and surveillance products, doorbells, voice recorders (Dictaphones), alarm clocks, flashlights, digital music players, calculators, calendars and planners, notepads, newspapers, TVs and TV remotes, DVDs and portable video players, landline internet, ATM / Debit / Credit Cards, credit card scanners, levelers, webcams, thermostats, light meters,

---

[24] Psalm 139:14; Jeremiah 31:3
[25] Proverbs 17:17, 18:24, 27:5-6; Ephesians 4:15
[26] Proverbs 14:10,13

barcode scanners, measuring tapes, USB thumb drives… And the list of what a smartphone can do just keeps growing.

All this power in your pocket!

People rely upon any number of the hundreds of apps on their smartphones to help them through each day. Users access their bank accounts and pay bills by cell phone app without needing to sit down by a desktop computer. Some people turn on and off house lights and other household appliances with them. Today, you can manage your washing machine remotely with your cell phone… although no one has quite figured out yet how to actually get your cell phone to put your clothes into the washing machine for you and remove them when the washing cycle is finished! There seems to be an app for just about anything and everything you could think of, need, or want. What a George Jetson[27] kind of life we lead today!

Even Baby Boomers have come to rely upon their mobiles and must think hard sometimes when answering the question, "What did you do before there were smartphones? How did you get along without them?"

Many of these modern conveniences indeed provide help to us, making many of the functions of our daily lives easier. However, they also come to us at the steep price of the loss of our personal privacy.

Think about how the smartphone manufacturers and app after app track our activities, likes, movement, and location every day. Are we becoming too desensitized when it comes to giving up our privacy? Where will it all lead going forward?

How Many Genders? Ze, Hir, Hirs

When I was a kid, we used to watch a TV show called, *Fantasy Island*. Today's Fantasy Island is not a TV show. It is everyday life for the Postmodernist.

---

[27] Google him for yourself in case you are too young to know who he is.

Take the word, gender, for example.

Before the word, gender, was taken over by Postmodern culture, it was defined and used in one of two very specific ways:

First and foremost, it simply means one of the two sexes: either male or female.[28] This most original definition is derived from the etymology of the word which is the Latin word, *genus*, meaning "to be born."

Secondly, it was (and still is) used in grammar to define nouns in languages such as French, German and Spanish as being either masculine, feminine, or neutral gender.

That's it! Period.

However, Postmodern culture hijacked this perfectly normal word and warped its definitions to include a whole slew of nonsensical meanings that allow people to create their own reality and live in their own Postmodern Fantasy Island.

One website lists 112 possible "gender identities" as of September 2019.[29] Facebook USA offers 58 gender designation options for users.[30] That number jumps to 71 for Facebook users in the U.K.[31]

New York City gives people a choice of 31 official gender identities and warns businesses in the city that they will face six-digit fines in violation of a U.N. Commission on Human Rights law if they do not comply.[32]

The State of California was the first in the nation to pass a law making it legal to identify oneself as "they," "them," or "it" instead of male or female on state issued IDs, Driver's Licenses, and birth certificates.[33]

I am not an "it" and in your heart of hearts, you know that you are not one either! The devil has even convinced *man* to invent new personal

---

[28] webstersdictionary1828.com/Dictionary/gender

[29] paradigmsanddemographics.blogspot.com/2019/09

[30] abcnews.go.com/blogs/headlines/2014/02/heres-a-list-of-58-gender-options-for-facebook-users

[31] telegraph.co.uk/technology/facebook/10930654/Facebooks-71-gender-options-come-to-UK-users

[32] dailycaller.com/2016/05/24/new-york-city-lets-you-choose-from-31-different-gender-identities

[33] esquire.com/news-politics/a13029632/california-recognizes-third-gender

pronouns such as, ze, hir and hirs, to replace the concrete pronouns that have worked just fine for 6,000 years, namely, he, she, him, her, his and hers. What an insult to the One Who created you and me and called us "fearfully and wonderfully made!"[34]

But this is life under Postmodernism.

Amen and A-woman

Postmodern liberal theology, political correctness, and "wokeness" are just so mixed up, to put it lightly!

On January 3, 2021, a Democrat representative from the State of Missouri (who is also allegedly an ordained minister in the theologically progressive United Methodist Church) ended his prayer in the U.S. Congress like this,

> **We ask it in the name of the monotheistic God, Brahma, and (the) god known by many names, many different faiths. Amen, and A-woman.**[35]

First of all, "Amen" is not a gender-related word. It is a word transliterated from Hebrew that confirms what has been prayed or said. It simply means, "certainly," "so it is," or more famously, "so be it." It has nothing whatsoever to do with gender. It is ridiculous to submerge this wonderful word into the mud and muddle of Wokeism.

Secondly, this is how far so-called Christian ministers who are steeped in liberal theology and political correctness will go in appeasing the gods of Postmodernism. Shameful.

In a Postmodern world, you are told that you can "identify" as anything you want. Why? Because Postmodernism convinces the gullible of the lie that there is no fixed, absolute truth, and no inviolable moral code to which they are accountable.

---

[34] Psalm 139:14

[35] globalnews.ca/news/7553949/amen-awomen-prayer-congress

Postmodern thought reasons this way:

"Right and wrong, good and evil, morality and immorality exist only as far as a person's own personal opinion about them. Moral standards are a matter of one's own interpretation. What is right or wrong to you is not necessarily right or wrong to me. Do not impose your standards on me. You must accept me as I am, meaning that you must approve of my (aberrant) lifestyle and, do not push your beliefs off on me!

"And, anyway, who knows if there is a sovereign, omnipotent, creator God to whom *man* is accountable? There might be such a God, but then again, maybe not. Who knows? Nobody knows anything for sure so just make your own reality."

The net result of this misguided philosophy of gobbledygook? Perversions of every unthinkable kind run rampant.[36]

Mr. and Mrs. Adam

Let's look at the meaning of the following words from Genesis 5:1-2 in the Strong's Hebrew Dictionary of Old Testament words:

1 This is the book of the generations of <u>Adam</u> (H121). In the day that God created <u>man</u> (H120), in the likeness of God made he him; 2 <u>male</u> (H2145) and <u>female</u> (H5347) created He them; and blessed them, and called their name <u>Adam</u> (H120), in the day when they were created.[37]

The definition for Strong's Hebrew word number H120 is "Adam" which is a transliteration of the Hebrew word.

אָדָם *'âdam, aw-dam'; from H119 ruddy; i.e. a human being (an individual or the species, mankind, etc.)*

Here are four uses for this word according to the Strong's Dictionary of Hebrew Words: [38]

---

[36] Judges 21:25

[37] KJV (emphasis added)

[38] Strong's Dictionary of Old Testament Hebrew Words

1. man (A human being of the male gender.)
2. man, mankind (People in general and much more frequently the intended sense in Old Testament.)
3. Adam, first man
4. a city in the Jordan valley

This word is used 552 times in the Old Testament. The vast majority of times this word is used in the Old Testament, it is used to refer to a group of people (both male and female, i.e.: the whole human race).

H121 is a derivative of H120 and is used only nine times in the KJV. It is always translated, "Adam" and refers to the first man (8x) and a city (1x) in the Jordan valley.

The Hebrew word for "male" in the Genesis verse above is Strong's number H2145 which means:

> רָכָר *zâkâr, zaw-kawr'; from H2142; properly, remembered, i.e. a male (of man or animals…):—× him, male, man(child, -kind).*

The Gesenius' Hebrew-Chaldee Lexicon says of this word,

as being he through whom the memorial of parents is continued.

The KJV translates Strong's H2145 eighty-one times total in the following manner: male (67x), man (7x), child (4x), mankind (2x), him (1x).

Finally, the Hebrew word translated "female" is H5347:

> הָרְבָב *nᵉqêbâh, nek-ay-baw'; from H5344; female (from the sexual form):—female.*

The KJV translates Strong's H5347 twenty-two times in the following manner: female (18x), woman (3x), maid (1x).

My point in examining these key words in Genesis 5:1-2 is two-fold:

First, is that the Hebrew word for "man", "men" and "mankind" not only refers to a male person but is also used for humanity as a whole or a specific group of people regardless of their gender, i.e.: *"mankind."*

The second point is that God only made two sexes or genders! Not 3 or 5 or 10 or 58 or 74! **Just two**: male and female.

The devil has convinced Postmodern *man* that each person has the right to decide if their gender feelings match or mismatch their biological sex at birth.

He has fed sinful *man* with the lie that it is perfectly normal for men to prefer other men and women to prefer other women... and *man* has eaten from this plate of lies.[39] But, these perversions in human relationships are only the appetizer of what is on the plate of poisonous perversion the devil has prepared for *man*.

With a clear refusal to accept any moral standards, the perverse activities of *mankind* grows from bad to worse.[40]

Follow the Science!

"Follow the science!" is the rally cry of Modernism and Postmodernism, but only when it fits their ideological narrative. When "the science" doesn't support their position, however, they rail against those who do "follow the science." The hypocrisy stinks.

It is clear that we are no longer truly in the Modern Era because the Modern Era focused completely on "the science" of everything. Way back in the Modern Era, only that which could be proven scientifically was to be believed. Anything that required faith and belief was totally rejected as nonsense and unreal. But now, Postmodernism has led humanity into so much confusion. Science, Biology, and even Mathematics are no longer fixed and objective disciplines anymore.

The ridiculously obvious, fixed and eternal answer to two plus two is four in a sane world. The answer has always been four since the dawn of time, but that is no longer the case in Postmodern culture. In

[39] Romans 1:21-27
[40] 2 Timothy 3:13

the Postmodern world, the answer to two plus two is whatever a person wants it to be! In the Postmodern world, absolutely nothing is absolute! Of course, the truth that most Postmoderns don't want to talk about is that they know very well that two plus two forever equals four and that it can equal no other number. They know that but they have to play along with the nonsense of Postmodern philosophy. Why? Because the goal is to destroy absolutes completely.

You can dress up a casket with the most beautiful flower arrangement in the world, but that will never change the fact that it is still a casket filled with a dead man's bones! [41]

In similar fashion, you can call an apple an orange all day long, but it is still an apple!

You can call the color red, blue all day long, but it is still the color red!

You can call an ugly wart-covered toad, a magnificent bald eagle all day long, but it is still an ugly wart-covered toad!

You get the picture… Follow the science!

Let's face it, a biological girl will *always* be a biological girl with XX chromosomes! And a biological boy will *always* be a biological boy with XY chromosomes! The chromosomes which fix the sex of the baby at conception *never change* no matter how one tries to dress up their sexual preference by using words, clothing, or medical procedures and therapies! Trying to do so is another example of how Postmodernism is living on Fantasy Island!

The science is clear: Chromosomes don't change! That is the *science!* And that is the inviolable, immutable *truth!*

Tell that to the Postmodernist the next time that he/she/it/they/ze/hir/hirs barks out the demand that you,

"Follow the science!"

---

[41] Matthew 23:27-28

Nothing written here is at all hateful towards people living aberrant lifestyles. It is just plain and simple truth and science. Sadly, so many are being hoodwinked by the devil, and this in abundance, through Modern-Postmodern philosophy and culture.

The only solution for every heart is Jesus Christ.[42]

My dad, for example, was born and raised in the Lutheran Church. He went to church every single Sunday growing up. He was baptized as a baby and then confirmed as a teenager according to the customs of the Lutheran Church. He never once drank alcohol, smoked or gambled growing up or as an adult. Not a single sip of alcohol. Not one puff of a cigarette. He was not a womanizer. In short, he had no "vices" throughout his life.

At the age of 26, he married my mom and remained a faithful husband and father the rest of his life. When he was thirty-six years old, he brought our family to Liberia, West Africa for three years because of his desire to serve God as a missionary (albeit as a lay missionary at that time under the Lutheran Church).

Upon our family's return to the U.S., he became deeply involved in the little country Lutheran Church that he had grown up in and was now raising his family. He became the pastor's right hand helper and served as president of the church council.

Yet, at the age of 42, with that good record to his credit, my dad knew that he wasn't right with God. My dad knew that if he died at that moment, he would have gone to hell. He was condemned in sin even though he was faithfully living an outwardly righteous life.

In church one Sunday, he cried out privately to God saying, "Jesus, I don't know if You are even real, but if You are, please do something in my life and in my heart because I am dying on the inside."

---

[42] Acts 4:12

He did not mean dying in the physical sense but rather in his heart of hearts, he knew he was spiritually lost. His status as a lifelong, baptized and confirmed member of the Lutheran Church and ex-missionary just could not provide him peace with God.

My dad got saved that day at the age of forty-two.

My point is that people living religious and/or moral lives are just as lost and in need of God's grace and salvation as the person living an aberrant, ruined life.

Without Christ, we are all sinners, for the Bible says that,

__all__ have sinned and fallen short of the glory of God.[43]

Here's the bottom line:

When God created man, He created them male and female (only two genders or sexes), blessed them (both) and called them (both) "man." God named them Male Adam and Female Adam or Mr. and Mrs. Adam. It was Adam who gave Eve her name.[44]

Here's something else to think about. The relationship between God and Israel was described more than once in analogous terms as husband and wife in the Old Testament books of prophecy.[45] Surely Scripture is not inferring that only the women of Israel were included in the description, "Jehovah's wife." Obviously, this analogous description covered the whole nation of Israel, males and females.

How about in the New Testament, where believers of both genders are also equally called "sons of God" [46] and the "bride of Christ?" [47]

Sure, women are sometimes referred to in masculine terms, (i.e.: *man, men, mankind,* and son of God), but let's also remember that men were

---

[43] Romans 3:23 (emphasis added)

[44] Genesis 3:20

[45] Isaiah 54:5; Jeremiah 2:2; 3:1,14

[46] Matthew 5:9; John 1:12; Romans 8:14; Galatians 4:6

[47] 2 Corinthians 11:2; Revelation 19:7-9; 21:2,9-11

included in God's description of His unfaithful "wife," Israel, in the Old Testament, and are called the "bride of Christ" in the New Testament. So why all the squawk about sexism and misogyny? It all washes out in the end!

Let's not conflate these occasions in God's Word describing various aspects of our relationship with God as being the same as the complete perversion of gender identity and terminology being practiced today. They are not the same.

In the Resurrection

Only in the afterlife does biological gender cease to be relevant.[48] For as long as we are still alive on this earth, girls are girls and boys are boys, period.

Let's not visit the blame for the perverted consequences of Adam's fall on a perfect, holy and loving God with Whom there is no distinction, favoritism, or discrimination when it comes to the worth of one sex over the other! [49]

The Infiltration of Postmodernism in the Church

It is no surprise that the world marches in lockstep with cultural conformity leading them straight into the vilest forms of perversion. What is troubling, though, is the impact that Postmodernism is having on Christianity. Postmodernism has had a significantly more devastating impact on Christianity than Modernism ever did.

In the transition from the Premodern to the Modern Age, the devil came at the Church with clear black and white choices:

"There is no God," screamed the Modernist!

But the more Modernism demanded subjection to atheism, the stronger the Church became, standing steadfast against such a ridiculous atheistic

---

[48] Matthew 22:30; Mark 12:25

[49] Job 34:19; Psalm 139:14; Acts 10:34-35; Romans 2:11; Galatians 3:28

notion. And then, almost as if realizing the ineffectiveness of his direct, frontal assault on Christianity using atheism, the enemy adapted an even more cunningly sinister approach in the ushering in of Postmodernism.

How to Kill a Frog

Do you know how to kill a frog? Everybody knows that if you try to put a frog in hot water, he'll jump right out (e.g., the Modern approach)! But, if you put him in a kettle of cool water and light the burner underneath, as the water begins to heat up gradually, the frog doesn't notice the rising water temperature.

By the time he does realize, "Hey! This water is getting hot!" It is too late! The water is beginning to boil and cook him to death. He is too weakened and powerless to jump out. He's cooked!

The tandem influences of Postmodern culture and liberal theology are the pot of slowly boiling water. Word-deficient believers are the unsuspecting frog who got into the water when it is cool and refreshing (when it is "cool" for the Church to mimic the world in the name of reaching the world) but ends up getting cooked. By the time the Word-deficient believer recognizes the dangers of mixing Postmodernism into their faith, they are already severely weakened, disillusioned, and drifting downstream with the rest of Postmodern society. They're cooked!

This is what is happening to much of the Church today.

Saints in Christ, beware! There are two philosophical warfronts to this fight of faith we are in. We are not just facing off against Modernism's, "God is dead. He doesn't exist," philosophy. The bulk of that era is already in the rearview mirror of history, although the residue of this war rages on.

This Postmodern Era is far more sly, cunning, and dangerous because the philosophy that drives it muddies the waters for everyone. At least with "God is dead," you can take the opposite position: "No, God is alive and really exists!"

But today, much of the Church is in a rut, trying to win the (spiritual) war of the past and yet is completely unaware that it has already acquiesced, in many ways, to the war of the present and future. Many Modernists and Christians are still fighting that older battle not realizing that humanity already moved on over the past 40-50 years to the Postmodern spiritual and cultural war for control of *man's* soul.

There are some very worrisome trends slipping into Christianity and church culture. These are polluting the Gospel message and drawing the hearts of many believers away from purity in Christ in favor of compromises, substitutes, and deceptions.

Postmodernism provides the stage upon which many Christians are now dancing (sometimes literally speaking) to the devil's pleasure. All the while believing the deception that the more they pattern and package their style after the world, somehow, the more attractive the Christian faith will be to the world.

Chapter Five

POSTMODERN CONTEXTUALIZATION OF THE GOSPEL

For the time will come when they will not endure sound doctrine; but wanting to have their ears tickled, they will accumulate for themselves teachers in accordance with their own desires, 4 and will turn away their ears from the truth and will turn aside to myths.

2 Timothy 4:3-4

It is Called "Contextualization of the Gospel"

Contextualization means different things to Evangelicals and the liberal, progressive streams of Christianity.

To Evangelicals, it became a keyword and practice among major world mission organizations over the past 40-50 years. Evangelicals use this word to describe their efforts in bringing the Gospel to an unreached group of people in a way that the target group can best understand it. However, what always remains of greatest importance to the missionary is the faithful delivery of the Gospel message without compromising any portion of it to make it more palatable to the local culture. Fidelity to the Word is of highest priority, not appeasement to local culture and customs.

Progressive, liberal theology also built a philosophical framework around this same word. In liberal theology, to contextualize the Gospel means to adapt the Gospel, its message and presentation, to its surroundings. This stream of theology believes that everything about belief in God and the Bible are constantly changing and evolving. Faith in God and interpreting the Word of God are to be adjusted and practiced through the lens of local contemporary cultural norms. Progressive theology does not believe in the infallibility and inerrancy of Scripture. According to progressive theology, Bible stories and miracles are not factual, historical events. They are just mythical beliefs and fairy tales. Disposable, in other words.

As I use the word, contextualization and its various forms, throughout the remainder of this book, the definition and context applied will be a mixture of liberal theology's definition of the word combined together with the failure within some Christian circles to hold to traditional Gospel fidelity and message integrity in favor of appeasing and aligning with contemporary culture.

The Catholic Church practiced its own brand of Gospel contextualization all over Central and South America and the Philippines, as Catholic explorers from Spain and Portugal colonized these areas of the world in past centuries. I lived in the Philippines for a dozen years and saw the result of this firsthand.

The pre-Spanish belief system in the Philippines was based on animism.

The religious life of the pre-Spanish Filipino was based on a fear of angering the spirit-world by violating taboo. These spirits were seen as hostile and waiting for any reason to inflict their wrath on people. The wrath of the spirit-world could come on a person because a spirit was hit by an object inadvertently thrown out of a window of the home at night, or by a woman hitting a spirit with a board used for

washing the clothes, palopalo. It was man's task to live in harmony with the spirit-world and by so doing, avoid gaba (curse) and receive panalangin (grace).

For the pre-Spanish Filipinos, spirit beings both inhabited nature and were one with nature. The spirits in control of the universe were what Westerners would call 'nature.' So, controlling the spirits in nature was the same as controlling nature. Though they lived in fear of the spirit-world, they also attempted to control it, and therefore nature, through the use of rituals, amulets, idols and other magical objects.[50]

As Spain colonized the islands, the Catholic Church sent over thousands of priests to introduce "Christianity" to the animistic nation. "Christian" teaching (the Spanish Catholic version of it anyway) was taught in the church... but the old animistic religion and spiritual worldview remained unchanged and was prominent in the home. The result was that the local animist beliefs and superstitions came to coexist side-by-side with Catholic worship in the Filipino worldview and daily life. This is still the case today.

Although Spanish Catholicism was the steady diet of the Filipino people for over 400 years, from the time Ferdinand Magellan landed in Cebu, Philippines in 1521, the modern-day Filipino --whether Catholic, Muslim and even Christian sometimes-- still has the pre-Spanish animistic beliefs firmly implanted in his or her personal worldview. This type of "folk Catholicism" was the result everywhere the Spanish and Portuguese explored and colonized.

These religious explorers and settlers practiced contextualization of the Gospel everywhere they went. With one hand, they loyally served up

---

[50] Filipino Spirit World by Rodney L. Henry, p. 8

generous portions of the Catholic doctrinal diet while on the other hand, quietly looked away as the natives they sought to convert continued to hold onto their pagan superstitions and worldview.

Contextualization of the Gospel is incapable of producing transformed lives because its intent is simply to throw a veil of Christianity over an existing belief system.

The consequence of the Catholic contextualization of the Gospel in the Philippines lingers today as expressed in a phrase I heard many years ago from a missionary there,

"Christianity in the Philippines is a mile wide but only an inch deep."

By contrast, the Western version of Catholicism (i.e.: North America and Western Europe) does not carry the same underlying infiltration of animism, blatant idolatry, and superstition. Its development and practice in the West more closely resemble mainstream Protestant Christianity. I believe this is largely due to the counter effects of the Reformation of the Church in the 16th century.

Outwardly, Catholicism shows its "brand," but when it comes to the packaging methods of its core structure, it much more resembles a chameleon: allowing animistic beliefs to remain underneath its exterior in the places it settled by the conquistadors of old, but using a different "color" in Europe and America where people were able to see and compare it to Protestantism.

Protestantism flourished in its early life because it delivered to the masses of Europe and America, a strong, uncompromised, and uncontextualized Gospel which was, both outwardly and inwardly, substantially different from Catholicism.

And the Race is on...

It is well known and documented that much of mainline Protestant denominationalism has devolved into a kind of lapdog for Modern and Postmodern theology since the start of the Modern Era. It kowtows to the shifting sands of culture, and conforms, contextualizes, and adjusts the Christian faith to whatever is culturally fashionable at any given time.

Until fairly recently, however, maybe only two or three decades at most, the Evangelical and Pentecostal/Full Gospel streams of Christianity vigorously opposed any attempt to contextualize the Gospel to the currents and whims of modern culture. To do so was (correctly) thought of as being gravely disloyal to the integrity of Scripture. These streams of Christianity steadfastly held to the sound principles of the supremacy of God's holy and infallible Word over all the affairs of life, believing it is our duty to conform our lives and morality to what the Word says, not the other way around.

Sadly, however, far too many Evangelical and Pentecostal/Full Gospel ministers and churches have also jumped onto the "we need to contextualize the Gospel to modern culture too" bandwagon in recent years. More and more justify using progressive contextualization methods in the name of making the Gospel more palatable to the world today. The thought process goes like this:

"We need to make the Gospel more attractive to this generation. We must adjust and adapt Christianity to fit the cultural norms of this generation."

This mindset is relatively new in Evangelical, Pentecostal and Full Gospel Christianity. It has resulted in a weakened Church which has abdicated its commission from the Head of the Church to be "salt and light"[51] and a "peculiar people."[52] Instead, the inevitable byproducts of this strategy are compromise and the lowering of the standards of godly living as clearly set forth in God's Word.

Evangelicals and Pentecostals have, in many cases, now begun to accept and normalize throwing that same thin veil of culturally contextualized Christianity over the lives of the unsaved in order to make them feel good

---

[51] Matthew 5:14-16

[52] 1 Peter 2:9

about coming to church, not unlike that which the conquistadors of old threw over the nations they conquered.

The Church has lost so much of its focus. The Postmodern priority is on how "cool" it can present itself to the world. It races ahead desperately trying impress the world by becoming as much like the world as possible in the name of attracting the world to the Christian faith. This fast-becoming mainstream push to assimilate modern culture into the practice of our faith is the result of the–infiltration of Postmodernism and progressive, liberal theology. First, having been adopted by mainline denominational Christianity. Now, this push to assimilate has also gained a firm foothold in Evangelical and Pentecostal Christianity. It has been a staple mindset for at least 25 years. It is hurting the cause of Christ and His Church.

In my more than 40 years of missions and full-time ministry at the time of this writing, I have seen and heard just about everything when it comes to the gimmicks, methods, and "packaging" used by ministers and churches.

Over the next four chapters, we will look at a few of the contextualized methods adapted by believers, ministers, and churches over the past 25-30 years, all in the name of "packaging the Gospel" in tinsel wrap that will not offend the world.

Chapter Six

THE EFFECTS OF POSTMODERNISM ON THE CHURCH - PART ONE

“

> *But realize this, that in the last days difficult times will come. 2 For men will be lovers of self, lovers of money, boastful, arrogant, revilers, disobedient to parents, ungrateful, unholy, 3 unloving, irreconcilable, malicious gossips, without self-control, brutal, haters of good, 4 treacherous, reckless, conceited, lovers of pleasure rather than lovers of God, 5 <u>holding to a form of godliness, although they have denied its power</u>; Avoid such men as these.*
>
> *2 Timothy 3:1-5 (emphasis added)*

How are Postmodern culture and contextualization of the Gospel influencing nearly all streams of Christendom today?

Let's find out.

My goal in writing is simply to spark awareness and to challenge all of us to prayerfully reconsider some of the methods of contextualization that are becoming deeply ingrained into the practice of our faith, and to see if their use is as genuinely effective as people have been led to think. Attempting to dismiss some of these practices merely as "style preferences" bearing no sufferable consequence to the core health of the

Christian Church simply does not work considering the current state of a large swath of Christianity in America and around the world today.

At least, let us take a hard look inwardly and honestly as to *why* we are doing what we are doing in church ministry today.

Emergent/Emerging Church Movement (ECM)

Much of the recent craze to adopt the world's cultural norms into Christianity was pushed in the 1990s and early 2000s by a movement known as the "Emergent Church Movement."

The Emergent Church Movement has diversified over the past twenty years into two broadly related camps.

The Emerg**ent** Church camp has developed into more of a settled organization of loosely connected churches with similar or compatible Emergent theology and philosophy.

The Emerg**ing** Church Movement has no fixed headquarters, no concrete organization or leadership. It is philosophical and ideological in nature. Its goal is to contextualize the Gospel to Postmodern culture. Although many Evangelical and Full Gospel churches disassociate themselves with the Emergent label, the fact remains that Emergent/Emerging ideology has influenced multiple streams of Christian faith and practice.

According to Wikipedia,

> **The emerging church is a Christian Protestant movement of the late 20th and early 21st centuries that crosses a number of theological boundaries: participants are variously described as Protestant, post-Protestant, evangelical, post-evangelical, liberal, post-liberal, socially liberal, anabaptist, reformed, charismatic, neo-charismatic, and post-charismatic. Emerging churches can be found throughout the globe, predominantly in North America, Brazil, Western Europe, Australia, New Zealand, and Africa... What those involved in the conversation mostly agree on is their disillusionment**

with the organized and institutional church and their support for the deconstruction of modern Christian worship, modern evangelism, and the nature of modern Christian community.[53]

Interestingly enough, the end of the above quote sounds eerily similar to the deconstruction efforts happening in so much of our civil society today as described in this transcribed quote from an interview with Trevor Louden[54] posted on the YouTube channel, *China in Focus*, on July 11, 2021. The following remarks are a bit disjointed at the start but he is answering a question from the interviewer about the tactics historically used by radicals to change societies and nations.

The quote of his answer, as transcribed, begins at the 23:23 minute mark:[55]

When you go back to the Chinese cultural revolution of the '60s. So when the Maoists took over, they did this in Cambodia cause that's symbols of the past. They're trying to create a new society so when they took over China, it took them a while to stamp out the old customs and the old traditions. And the cultural revolution of the '60s was the final push to get rid of the history and the culture and the old ways of China. So you had young kids, six, seven years old denouncing their parents, burning books, teenagers rampaging through the streets dragging professors around and torturing them, ripping down statues, destroying art works. They were eliminating everything.

---

[53] en.wikipedia.org/wiki/Emerging_church

[54] Trevor Louden is an author, filmmaker, and public speaker from New Zealand. For more than 30 years, he has researched radical left, Marxist, and terrorist movements and their covert influence on mainstream politics.

[55] https://youtu.be/H2MaOn4ZkFc

In Cambodia, they killed everybody with glasses, eyeglasses, because if you had eyeglasses, you must be an intellectual and they didn't want intellectuals because they have old ideas. They had to wipe out the whole <u>intellectual class</u> to have a lump proletariat of <u>peasants and farmers</u> that they could then mold into <u>a new society</u>. So every old form of speech had to be suppressed. Every old symbol had to be eliminated.

If you replace the phrase "intellectual class" with "elderly," and the phrase, "peasants and farmers," with "under 35 and inexperienced," and "a new society" with "new church norms," you would have a perfect description of Emerging Christianity. Different contextual worlds, but the same spirit behind both? Yes.

The point in drawing a parallel from this quote to what has been happening in Emergent-influenced Christianity is the emphasis on the *deconstruction* of anything and everything that represents ways and traditions long held to be important to the practice of Christian faith. Progressive, liberal theology and ECM ideology have been attempting to infiltrate every stream of Christianity and accomplish in similar fashion, the deconstruction of Bible-based Christianity, its forms, culture, customs, and values for decades now.

GotQuestions.org further explains,

The emerging, or emergent, church movement takes its name from the idea that as culture changes, a new church should emerge in response. In this case, it is a response by various church leaders to the current era of post-modernism. Although post-modernism began in the 1950s, the church didn't really seek to conform to its tenets until the 1990s. Post-modernism can be thought of as a dissolution of 'cold, hard fact' in favor of 'warm, fuzzy subjectivity.' The

emerging / emergent church movement can be thought of the same way.

The emerging / emergent church movement falls into line with basic post-modernist thinking—it is about experience over reason, subjectivity over objectivity, spirituality over religion, images over words, outward over inward, feelings over truth. These are reactions to modernism and are thought to be necessary in order to actively engage contemporary culture.[56]

When Emerging church philosophy takes over a church, the elderly are the first to be set aside and pushed out.[57] Elderly believers are either encouraged to leave their church, or worse yet, they are driven out of their home church. But why? Because in the Emergent world, they represent "old-fashioned, intolerant, and irrelevant" Christianity. In ECM ideology, the elderly are seen as remnants of the Premodern view and practice of Christianity. They are an impediment to the overall goals of ECM for a church.

This happened to the Lutheran Church I grew up in.

Several years ago, a young, fresh-out-of-seminary, Emergent trained ideologue was hired as the pastor of the Lutheran Church I grew up in.

It is clear that the church did not know what Emergent ideology was when they hired this man, and oh my, how that small country church paid the price for their mistake!

Within the first few weeks of him taking over, he drove out the organist who had been serving the Lord with her musical skills in that church since I was a child growing up there 50 years ago. She was the

---

[56] gotquestions.org/emerging-church-emergent

[57] 9marks.org/article/emerging-church-primer

choir director when I was still in grade school. Linnea[58] was in her early eighties when the ideologue was hired but he fought her tooth and nail on every level until he succeeded in driving her from the church she had served the Lord in for more than 50 years!

Next, one elderly member after another was made to feel unwelcome in the only church that they had attended for decades. Some of these families went back two and three generations or more in the church. But that was of no consequence to this outsider. He had no respect for the legacy of the families and generations he had been hired to serve. Instead, he tore apart one custom and family after another leaving the very fabric of the congregation in tatters.

Within three years, 70% of those over the age of fifty had been driven out of the church. Some, in the meanest sort of ways. Good people that I had known as a child, including Linnea, who were by that time in the sunset years of their lives, had become "persona non grata" in the only church they had ever known and belonged to. They were a generation of faithful church members who had kept the church buoyed for decades upon decades with their volunteerism and finances. But in a span of just 3-4 short, but emotionally turbulent years, all that they knew and loved, church-wise, was ripped from their lives. This "pastor" was determined to turn my childhood home church into an Emergent church, and sadly, for the most part, he succeeded.

He used his position to manipulate and influence the generations thirty-five and under to take over the church from the "outdated" elderly. Then, with the younger generation under his Emergent spell, he convinced the small country church to vote to stay in the ELCA synod after the synod had voted to accept LGBTQwxyz people as clergy.

In the end though, after five tumultuous years, he overplayed his hand and was fired.

---

[58] Her real name has been changed to protect the privacy of her family.

Our family goes back three generations in that small country Lutheran Church. My dad was born and raised in that church and had been a part of it his entire life. My parents raised my brothers and me there. They tried to comfort their friends as they were pushed out one-by-one by this Emergent minister, but eventually my parents were made to feel so unwelcome and were pushed out to.

Every time they would update me on the latest happenings, their stories sounded like scenes from a Frank Peretti novel.[59]

Those who had been pushed out did not return even after the man was fired. The sense of betrayal and hurt ran too deep. That small country church has never been the same after the tornado-like destruction that Emergent man wreaked upon it.

Only people under the age of thirty-five or forty, at most, are important in an Emergent/Emerging church. I have seen this pattern play out over and over in many churches in America and Europe. The younger the demographic of the church, the more successful that church is thought to be. The problem with this ideology is that one day that young and "acceptable" generation of today will eventually grow into the wrong age demographic. Then what?

Each local church develops a culture of its own over time. It behooves every local church to establish a culture and style that is stable enough to weather every passing church trend and provide a welcome to every generation.

Although the ECM movement no longer garners the spotlight in Christian news, its ideology and methods have already become integral to the contextualized approach taken in much of church ministry today. The residue of the damage it wrought on churches, individual lives, and to the practice of our Christian faith in the 21st century continues and cannot be overstated.

---

[59] Author of the famous fictional novels, "This Present Darkness" and "Piercing the Darkness" (Recommended reading by this author.)

Chasing the Stars

Another ailment of the Postmodern Church is how the Christian culture mentality has confused "big and flashy" as meaning "successful and anointed." Too many people think that size and fame are the measures for anointing and success. This is also hurting the Body of Christ today. We will deal with this topic in greater detail later in the book.

When "big names" and "big ministries" in the Body of Christ attain star power in the eyes of vulnerable, Postmodern feelings-based, Word-deficient sheep, the pressure becomes tremendous to always come up with something even bigger, more "anointed," more appealing, and more seductive, figuratively-speaking, to hold the interest of their audience.

Every multi-million dollar church and ministry faces fierce competition for people's attention and finances. This means that the pressure to constantly produce the next big thing or the next new revelation is great as well.

Why do Christians seem to need famous names, gimmicks, an angle or a label attached to something before they see it as being "anointed?" Why is the Church constantly captivated by anything new and shiny?

By heaven's metrics, *big and flashy* is not at all automatically synonymous with successful and anointed. Heaven does not calculate such weighty matters the way *men* do here on earth.

True, we cannot judge the hearts and intentions of *men*, but Jesus did tell us that we would recognize the quality of a person or ministry by its fruit.[60] If we really know the Word and our Lord, we should be able to discern, judge, and recognize what is from the heart of God and what is not. God doesn't need gimmicks![61]

Once again, however, the influence of Postmodern philosophy and liberal theology on the cultural temperament of the Postmodern believer

---

[60] Matthew 7:15-20; I Corinthians 3:12-15

[61] Proverbs 21:2

today has blunted the ability of many Christians in the Postmodern era to distinguish between the ploys of *men* and the Word of God.[62]

We must be aware that the closer we draw to the end of the age, the crazier and crazier the gimmicks, angles, and shiny new revelations will become. Sadly, too big a cut from the worldwide Body of Christ buys into all the nonsense.

Keep it simple

Second Corinthians 11:3 says,

3 But I am afraid that, as the serpent deceived Eve by his trickery, your minds will be led astray from sincere and pure devotion to Christ.

Keep your Christianity simple. Resist the temptation to constantly yearn after the newest cool, the newest vision or revelation, the newest best seller, the newest conference topic, the newest trend in church culture, etc. in the Church world. Let's stop blindly adoring big name preachers because of their fame.

There are tens of thousands of godly, sincere, hard-working small church pastors around the world who are too often overlooked and taken for granted by star-gazing saints sitting in the pews... or shall I say Emerging sofas!

There is wisdom for us in such simple verses as,

11 and to make it your ambition to lead a quiet life and attend to your own business... [63]

True faith in Christ is characterized by simplicity, sincerity and purity. There is a warning in 2 Timothy about what will happen to believers who refuse to listen to sound doctrine and wholesome teaching:

---

[62] 1 John 4:1-6

[63] 1 Thessalonians 4:11

3 For a time is coming when people will no longer listen to sound and wholesome teaching. They will follow their own desires and will look for teachers who will tell them whatever their itching ears want to hear. 4 They will reject the truth and chase after myths.[64]

Four consequences await those who refuse to listen to sound doctrine and wholesome teaching:

One, "they will follow their own desires."

Two, they "will look for teachers who will tell them whatever their itching ears want to hear."

Three, "they will reject the truth."

And four, they will "chase myths."

Look at the general state of Christians in all sorts of churches today, as well as those who have quit going to church all together, and you will find all four of these points of consequence operating in abundance.

But more importantly still, may each of us examine our own heart to make sure these four points are not found there!

Spirituality but not Church, Please

Also symptomatic of the Postmodern, Post-Christian era are the many Christians who have become disillusioned with church life.

One need be just a moderate consumer of current events to see news report after news report online today about the dwindling role of "organized church ministry" in people's lives. There is so much danger in this trend.

Throughout American history, for example, church attendance and relevancy consistently ranged between 70-80%. But, just twenty years into the new century and millennium, the percentage of self-identified

---

[64] 2 Timothy 4:3-4 NLT

Christians who attend church regularly or think that church is relevant to their lives has plummeted to below 40%. Possibly much lower than that. Is it mere coincidence that it was during this same time period that the Church scrapped many long-held values governing the practice of our faith in favor of adapting Postmodern contextualization methods and ECM styles? Did the adaption of these new forms stop or even slow the decline?

The Church should be alarmed by these statistics. However, the answer to them is *not* simply a Church that assimilates more to the world by looking, acting, and talking more like it!

In our Postmodern world, too many people who self-identify as Christian want Christianity without church, and spirituality without it being based exclusively on Christianity. [65]

There are two main kinds of "de-churched" Christians today as a result of Postmodern culture.

A "de-churched" Christian is someone who has stopped attending church regularly. Find a Postmodern de-churched Christian and you'll find someone well on their way to checking off all four points of consequence mentioned above from Second Timothy chapter four.

The first kind of de-churched Christian are those who think of themselves squarely as Christian but have dropped out of any kind of regular church attendance. This is the group that has become completely disillusioned with churches.

The top reason that people leave a church is unresolved personal conflict. This might be connected to a negative church experience. Other times, it is totally unrelated. Either way, sadly, for some it is just easier to cut and run. To them, church is expendable. They would rather leave the church than to deal with matters of pride, offense, worldliness,

---

[65] barna.com/churchless; barna.com/research/meet-love-jesus-not-church; barna.com/research/changing-state-of-the-church

and stubbornness in their own hearts. It's easier to blame others than to examine self. This is particularly characteristic of Millennials, Gen Z-ers, and heavily indoctrinated Postmoderns in general, where all forms of discomfort are to be avoided at all cost and where commitment and accountability are disposable commodities. They have decided they can be better Christians on their own than in belonging to a home church.

This is very unfortunate because Biblical Christianity is meant to be lived out in church communities. That is the model given to us in the New Testament.

From the Head of the Church to the gathering of the believers in the Upper Room in Acts chapters one and two, to the nine New Testament letters written to local churches (16 if you include the general epistles), to the customized messages of the Lord Jesus Christ to the seven churches of the Book of Revelation, the role and importance of the local church to the believer's fruitfulness and spiritual development is undeniable.[66]

The second kind of unchurched, self-identified Postmodern Christian strives for self-made spirituality. They would be offended if someone would call them unchristian, yet their belief system is not limited to Biblical truth and instruction. They are also open to other streams of belief and philosophy. They have no problem mixing paranormal experiences into their own self-designed brand of Christianity or looking to Eastern religions like New Age, Buddhism, and Hinduism to enhance their version of spirituality. To them, Christianity is just one of many sources for spiritual enlightenment.

Morally, the second kind of de-churched "Christian" supports everything pushed by secular Postmodern "woke" culture: living together outside the bond of marriage, aberrant lifestyles, social justice issues, and every other worldly activity. In their eyes, to engage in these activities and alternative lifestyles are just part of modern-day life. They

---

[66] Matthew 16:18; Acts 1-4; Hebrews 10:24-25

have convinced themselves that their behavior and lifestyles do not have anything to do with whether or not they are a "good" person. To them, it is the person who believes in spiritual and moral absolutes that should be considered old-fashioned, judgmental, unspiritual, unkind, and unchristian. Instead, they believe that their acceptance, tolerance, and non-judgment of anything the Bible calls "sin" is what makes them kinder and more spiritual than Bible-based, church-going believers who hold to Biblically fixed morals of right and wrong.

De-churched and unchurched Postmodern Christians see Biblical Christianity and church involvement as a stumbling block and irrelevant to their lives. They prefer to sit at home and watch the preaching of their choice on TV and YouTube. But that is precisely what Paul warned us against doing in Second Timothy chapter four. Picking and choosing messages that makes one feel good but never challenges, describes to a "t" the spiritual condition of those who have discarded belonging to a home church:

"They follow their own desires,

"they look for teachers who will tell them whatever their itching ears want to hear,

"they reject the truth," and they,

"chase myths."

Let's make use of the blessing of ministry by media where it makes sense: for the elderly and shut-ins who cannot make it to church, and for those living in far-flung areas or countries where no churches are available. For the rest of us, though, let's get up from our easy chair and go to church![67]

Spiritual and character growth take place as we share our lives in the local church. The saying is true that there is no perfect church. Small churches. Medium-size churches. Big churches. Mega churches. Each

---

[67] Psalm 122:1

church size has its own set of challenges and struggles. Each church size also offers its own set of strengths and advantages.

Don't wait until you find "the perfect church." Stop making your demand of finding a "perfect church" your excuse for not going to church at all. First of all, there is no such thing as "the perfect church" because we are all imperfect. The Bible says that we sharpen each other in the same way that iron sharpens iron.[68] Through friendship relationships in the local church, we learn humility, selflessness, commitment, accountability, giving and forgiving. But such characteristics are not vogue in Postmodern culture, leaving the unchurched person to choose a more comfortable, self-medicating kind of spirituality instead. This runs contrary to the set-up found in God's Word for the believer, pastor, and local church as expressed in these verses:

Ephesians 4:11-16 says,

> *11 And __He gave__ some as apostles, some as prophets, some as evangelists, some as __pastors and teachers__, 12 for the equipping of the saints for the work of ministry, for the building up of the body of Christ; 13 __until__ we all attain to the unity of the faith, and of the knowledge of the Son of God, to a mature man, to the measure of the stature which belongs to the fullness of Christ. 14 __As a result, we are no longer to be children, tossed here and there by waves and carried about by every wind of doctrine__, by the trickery of people, by craftiness in deceitful scheming; 15 but speaking the truth in love, __we are to grow up__ in all aspects into Him who is the head, that is, Christ, 16 from whom the whole body, being fitted and held together by what every joint supplies, according to the proper working of each individual*

---

[68] Proverbs 27:17

part, causes the growth of the body for the building up of itself in love.

And from Hebrews 10:24-25,

24 and let us consider how to stimulate one another to love and good deeds, 25 not forsaking our own assembling together, as is the habit of some, but encouraging one another; and all the more as you see the day drawing near.

It is abundantly clear in Scripture that Christianity is meant to be lived out in the context of a Word-based, loving local church setting. Serious disciples of Jesus Christ should be in them when possible, not self-medicating, figuratively speaking, at home.

Only since the turnover to the 21st century has the percentage of unchurched Christians risen and church attendance dropped so significantly.[69]

Personally, I believe that is an indictment against the presumed effectiveness of the contextualized methods being pushed so pervasively in Christianity today. Let's face it, the methods of "be-likeness" and contextualization that the Church has employed over the past 20-30 some odd years have not produced the promised results of a greater harvest, nor have they resulted in a stronger generation of more spiritually and morally stable believers and churches. The rest of this chapter outlines some of those methods, calling into question their effectiveness.

Cancelling Jesus

For a little over two decades, Emergent-influenced churches have adjusted every facet of their church set up, from the physical arrangement in their church to the construction of their church services, all in a

---

[69] barna.com/research/changing-state-of-the-church

desperate attempt to claim relevancy and acceptance from Postmodern society. Following in lockstep with the world, the Emerging-laced Postmodern Church is now trying to attract and impress Postmoderns, Millennials, and Gen Z-ers by offering them a Christianity that looks as much like their unsaved world as possible.

First of all, by shortening the church service to accommodate the diminished capacity of Postmodern *man's* microwave attention span. Many church services today are geared to accommodate the busy life of the Millennial. Should the preaching last longer than the waiting time in a fast food drive-through lane, the preacher has gone on way too long. That may be an exaggeration, but the point is made. Short-term appeal is too often taking precedence over the long-term development of well-equipped disciples of Jesus Christ in some churches.

Secondly, by designing and programming the Sunday service more to impress and entertain, rather than as an important, spiritual gathering of God's people. In some cases, the praise and worship time has begun to look more like a weekly concert rather than an inviting moment for believers to corporately exercise their priestly rights, duties, and privileges in worshipping God.[70]

Thirdly, some churches have come to rely heavily on special effects optics such as laser lights, fog machines, and a darkened sanctuary to set the Postmodern mood apart from the more historical atmosphere of a church sanctuary on Sunday morning.

Of course, who cares about these things since they do not have direct impact on the long term development of disciples of Jesus Christ, right? Or is it possible they do indeed bear partial, if even indirect, responsibility for the current state of the declining numbers in Christianity, and the increase in numbers of morally compromised and theology-deficient Christians today? Where is the evidence they

---

[70] 1 Peter 2:5-9; Ephesians 5:19; Colossians 3:16; 1 Corinthians 14:26

have had a direct impact on the stabilization or increase of Christianity in quality or quantity? Let's not be afraid to ask the questions. Every poll and study on the current condition of Christianity reveals a Church more theologically deficient, morally compromised, and less attended than was the case for hundreds of years, prior to the implementation of so many Postmodern contextualized style and method adjustments.

Fourth, pulpits and lecterns have also been "cancelled" in the Emerging version of "cancel culture." Altars, pulpits and lecterns are thought to be a "turn-off" to Millennials and Postmoderns coming to church, so a bistro table has become the modern-day pulpit. Once again, I am not saying that using a bistro table as the preacher's pulpit is wrong or sinful. Go ahead and use a bistro table if you want. Knock yourself out. A table, an altar, a lectern, a pulpit? Who cares? They are just pieces of furniture, right? In the Old Testament, God cared very much about the furniture in His tabernacle and temples. But, of course, those things were imperfect shadows which spoke of Christ and were fulfilled in Christ. As a missionary, I have held services in all kinds of places including under trees because the believers had no building at all to meet in, so I am not being legalistic about furniture. I'm only challenging us to question why altars, pulpits and lecterns are no longer acceptable.

Fifth, another style change that has become standard since the 1990s is the practice of having professionally produced PowerPoint presentations, etc. to guide the congregation through the pastor's message. While this is not a major issue, my point in mentioning it has to do more with the side of the preacher and the development of the future generation of preachers. How are we, as a senior generation of preachers and ministers, mentoring those coming up behind us?[71]

[71]Exodus 13:14; Deuteronomy 6:7,20-25; 32:7; Psalm 71:18; 78:4-6; 145:4

Are we pushing them deeper into the contextualized Postmodern pit or offering them a model based on the standard found in 1 Corinthians 2:4-5?

> *4 and my message and my preaching were not in persuasive words of wisdom, but in demonstration of the Spirit and of power, 5 so that your faith would not rest on the wisdom of mankind, but on the power of God.*

The point is lost if the reader thinks this author is advocating against the use of modern technology in the church. I am neither anti-modern nor anti-technology. Allow me to illustrate my point this way:

When I began to call on some of our young adults who have graduated from Bible School to preach a Sunday service or fill-in for me in my absence, I gave them this restriction,

"You may not use PowerPoint (or other beamer related) presentations when you preach the Sunday service. I want you to be competent in the Word of God and learn what it means to depend on the Holy Spirit for your anointing. Understand what it takes to hold a congregation for a 45-60 minute message without depending on manmade crutches."

They have thanked me for guiding them this way.

Back in the 1990s, most churches that had long relied upon overhead projectors for providing song lyrics to their congregations transitioned to beamers. Along with that transition came worship song and Bible projection software. What a blessing these tools are!

I would venture to estimate that 90% plus of all churches began right away to beam the Scripture verses used by the pastor during the preaching hour. Beaming verses has been the standard ever since.

However, the Lord led me to a different approach in our church. We did indeed begin to use a beamer for our praise and worship song lyrics transitioning away from the overhead projector; yet, I told the head of our Soundbooth Ministry not to beam the Bible verses I use during preaching and explained my reasons to both our Soundbooth and to our congregation,

"If we beam the verses up on the screen, then you will stop bringing your own Bibles to church. It is important that you bring your own Bible, read your own Bible, and highlight in your own Bible during the preaching. Have a strong relationship with God through your own Bible."

Sure enough! Today, some twenty years into beamer church life, if I randomly ask who brought their Bibles to church on any given Sunday, about 70% or more of our congregation will raise their (real book, not mobile device) Bible into the air... every time! Glory to God! When there are visitors in our service, it is not uncommon for a believer to move next to them during the preaching in order to share their Bible with the visitor.

Sixth, church pews and chairs arranged in the traditional sanctuary fashion are also cancelled in Emergent churches for being too "religious" and uncool! Some Emerging-influenced churches have gone so far as to fill their sanctuaries with sofas, easy chairs, coffee, and bistro tables to stand or sit around, so the attender can plug in their mobiles and enjoy their cup of joe during the service. Some churches also offer non-alcoholic beer bars that people can run over to for a quick drink before or after the service. The Emergent way is to set up the sanctuary and its atmosphere to mimic a Starbucks restaurant.

Since the '90s, "cool" has become what is all-encompassing and important in an Emerging, Postmodern church! In the mind of the Emergent-laced, Postmodern Church, all "old church norms" must be torn down because they are seen as barriers to the Postmodern generation.

Finally, about 20-25 years ago, at the start of Emergent influence on church culture, it also became fashionable for pastors, worship leaders and anyone who stands on the stage to come as casually dressed as possible for church (to put it lightly). Out the window went the Premodern church culture of giving effort to look our best as a respect for the presence of

God and His house. This long-held custom survived the Modern Era, only to be ditched in the Postmodern Era.

In like fashion, wearing a Christian tat on one's arm also became an essential part of the Emerging Postmodern preacher's accessories. I have actually heard Christians say that a believer without a tattoo can never successfully lead someone to Christ who has one. How ridiculous is that reasoning? The message that saves from sin and eternal separation from God does not hinge on manmade skin ink. Just think of where that road leads... Jesus Himself would need to be cancelled. Jesus Himself would be disqualified because He has no tat... only the scars which remain as an eternal testimony of the price He paid in purchasing our redemption.

The Bible says,

> *1 There is therefore now no condemnation to them which are in Christ Jesus, who walk not after the flesh, but after the Spirit.*[72]

When a person comes to Christ, already bearing the marks or consequences of decisions made in their pre-Christ life, this verse brings comfort and assurance. However, what Postmodernism has sold to the Church concerning "Christian tattoos" and lots of other worldly likenesses which are being pushed as essential to church ministry need a rethink.

Are "Christian tattoos" what God had in mind when He instructed us to present our bodies as a living and holy sacrifice?

> *19 Or do you not know that your body is a temple of the Holy Spirit who is in you, whom you have from God, and that you are not your own? 20 For you have been bought with a price: therefore glorify God IN [not "on"] your body.*[73]

---

[72] Romans 8:1 KJV (emphasis added)

[73] I Corinthians 6:19-20 (emphasis and brackets added)

And again in Romans 12:1-2 (emphasis added),

> *Therefore I urge you, brethren, by the mercies of God, to* <u>*present your bodies a living and holy sacrifice,*</u> *acceptable to God, which is your spiritual service of worship. 2 And do not be conformed to this world, but be transformed by the renewing of your mind, so that you may prove what the will of God is, that which is good and acceptable and perfect.*

Sacred Cows

Granted, all seven of the foregoing points are, for the most part, matters of pastoral and church leadership taste and style preference. They are not, by themselves, the main point but rather are given as examples of the kinds of alterations that have taken place in the practice of our faith in just the last 25-30 years due to Postmodern influence over the Church. I do not infer that any church using the aforementioned points has automatically lost the substance of the Gospel message. Rather, the focus of this book is in asking the "big picture" questions, such as:

What will happen if the Church continues full-steam-ahead down the path of Postmodern contextualization and cultural adaptation, always adjusting the practice of our faith in order to align it with whatever the current culture dictates as we go deeper into the 21st century? What will Christianity and church services look like in another 30-40 years if the Church continues to prioritize the cultural adaptation and contextualization of the faith we hold dear? Will there be any lasting semblance of a church service as we have known it considering the abject importance the Church has placed on using the ever-evolving styles and methods that are ticklish to the world in Postmodern times? Will there be anything left of the practice of our faith that is still recognizably, scripturally, solidly Christian? What are we passing on to those who follow in our footsteps? Remember the lesson of the slowly cooked frog?

I believe that it is vital for the Church to ask and answer these questions lest culture and the ways of the world answer them for us! True, our faith is resilient but its resilience is *despite* the Church's rush to contextualize, not because of it.

The Emergent-influenced Postmodern Church distorts and misrepresents who the Jesus of the Bible is in order to keep Him. When that doesn't fly, He is simply cancelled altogether.

An alternative title that could have been given to this chapter is, "Don't Touch My Sacred Cows,"[74] simply because any query into the Postmodern cultural norms used in Christianity has been fended off and labeled as being judgmental and nitpicking. We are trained now not to question but merely to accept and follow.

I understand that the foregoing seven points and many other similar points made in this book will be vigorously defended as merely points of style, preference, and method, not substance.

"Style and methods are of zero consequence (that's just packaging). As long as we are remaining faithful to the message, that is all that is important." This is the line of defense from the contextualized Christian.

Yet, where is the proof that these contextualized methods are producing better results than the way we practiced our faith before the transition into the 21st century? Statistics on the current state of Christianity in the Postmodern West reveal quite the opposite. In fact, statistics show that churches were indeed fuller and more well attended before the deconstruction of Premodern church norms and adaptation of contextualized methods began in the 1990s. Is there a connection?

Perhaps in past generations and eras the diversity of styles and methods was not problematic, but we are living in a very different day. Style and methods do matter because in many ways their use and the

---

[74] merriam-webster.com/dictionary/ sacred cow definition: "something that is often unreasonably immune from criticism or opposition"

defense of their use have practically become the more important part of the conversation. And, the problem with that is that many of the styles, methods and standards being employed today are all-too-often producing disciples that better mimic and mirror Postmodern culture and philosophy instead of teaching them how to stand up to it and stand apart from it.

Perhaps the seven points above *are* "just style points" that do not interfere with substance, perhaps. Perhaps none of them are wrong or dangerous by themselves, perhaps. But, shall we forever blindly run after every passing "cool" trend of the world, looking for ways to incorporate these into the practice of our Christian faith without so much as asking ourselves and the Lord, "Is this a good idea, Lord?" Maybe the message does suffer some after all?

Rather than state an opinion, I will leave the reader with this question, "Could these things and the fierce and unquestioning defense of their use be sacred cows in Christianity today?" The author asks only that the reader ask themselves.

I believe there are many reasons for the diminished influence of today's Church in society: the breakdown of the nuclear family, the removal of God, prayer, and the Ten Commandments from schools and public spaces over the past 60 years, the influence and impact of secular and social media, etc. However, one likely culprit in my humble opinion are the contextualized compromises the Church has made over the past 20-30 years to appease and cater to culture, Post-modernizing all things Christian. Is it possible that the Church is now beginning to reap some unintended consequences of its embrace of these contextualized methods over the past quarter of a century and its love of all things popular and fashionable?

Hip Hop Didn't Work...

In my 40-plus years of ministry, 28 of which so far have been serving as pastor, I made one regrettable attempt at trying to gain the lives of the teenagers in our church for Christ through Postmodern methods. The story goes like this:

For twelve years, from 1996 until about 2008, being relatively new at pastoring and against my better judgment, I allowed the first two youth directors in our young church to use Christian Hip Hop music and dance as a primary focus and method of youth group activity for the teenagers. The stipulation I gave the youth leaders in our young church was that the music had to be Christian, not worldly. Our first two youth leaders assured me that this was the right way to reach the teens and secure them for Christ.

Well, the kids started dancing in 1996. Each generation of teenagers that grew up in our church during that period came to our youth meetings, danced to Christian Hip Hop and were even excited and willing to present their dances at church events. Of course, some devotional teachings and Bible exhortations were also given in each youth meeting... but the emphasis remained on Christian Hip Hop. And, for twelve years, we lost youth after youth to the world by the age of 18! None stayed. The teens "put up with" the Bible stuff in order to get to the dancing they craved. They didn't know or care what the words of the songs were, it was the Hip Hop music and dance they were after.

We fed their flesh, and for twelve years, each batch of teens ate it up and then promptly left Christ and church anyway. We lost generation after generation for twelve solid years as we employed a method that contextualization laid claim to in church culture as a ringer for success. Although I was never at peace in allowing the youth leaders to use this method during those twelve years, I did not understand at the time that I was actually caving to Postmodern contextualization methods.

Finally, in 2008, our church purchased and moved into a new building. Coincidentally, the youth director changed at the same time, and we charted a new course for our youth ministry.

I told the new youth director to stop the Hip Hop and focus on feeding our youth with God's Word. The results have been piling up ever since.

Some youth still choose the world by the time they turn 18, but since we refocused the methods and priorities of our youth meetings in 2008, more and more youth are remaining faithful to Christ and staying in church.

In our case, the *results* between these two very opposite *styles and packaging* of youth ministry are as evident as night and day.

Except for this one failed experiment in catering to culture rather than sticking with the Word, our church has steered clear by design from all of the seven points I outlined earlier.

A few years ago, a director in one of the three ministerial organizations I am credentialed with told me, "Karen, I love coming to your church because everything about it is so decent and in order from the time you walk in the door."

To God be the glory!

I firmly believe that a church can be modern, relevant, and effective without going full-blown Emergent/ Emerging, contextualized, and Postmodern.

I believe it is important that the Church begins now to steady its own ship so that we might pass on to future generations of preachers and disciples of Christ, a practice of faith which has maintained its independence from every cultural influence.[75]

Although we are not a large church, our membership demographic covers multiple generations, races and nationalities. It includes representation from every sociological generation. We have Elders, Boomers (I am a Boomer), Gen X-ers, teenagers, school-aged children and babies. We even have representation from the demographic group that a church like ours is not supposed to be effective in reaching namely, Millennials and Gen Z-ers. We have families and singles, glory to God! Some of our Gen Z-ers, Millennials, and teenagers serve faithfully and enthusiastically in various

---

[75] Deuteronomy 6:7,20-25; Psalm 78:4-6

areas of church ministry. I love to see them walk into church every Sunday looking sharp and happy about it!

We encourage members from across the generational spectrum to contribute from their time, talents, and gifts. Each generation has something special to bring! We love the mingling of generations and keep compartmentalization of generations and other demographic groups within the body to a minimum.

All praise to the Head of the Church, Jesus Christ!

Focus on "Social Justice"

The Church is sidetracked! Focusing on Wokeness, politics, and social issues have become part of the new vogue in some corners of Christendom.

The Biblical and historical nature of Christianity is to focus its priorities, energy, and resources on that which directly propagates the Gospel in the world, for example: evangelism, missions, Bible Schools, Bible translation, church planting and church ministry, etc.

In recent years, however, a monumental shift has taken place within Christendom. Today, social, cultural, and political issues have become the focus of many churches. Activism, in other words. Emergent-laced churches crave acceptability from the world. This is in direct opposition to Jesus' instruction for us to be salt and light.[76]

The Postmodern Church is so busy giving time and energy to these culturally trendy social issues, trying to gain acceptability from secular Postmodern culture, while at the same time obediently muffling and diluting the actual message of the cross, reasoning that a straightforward Gospel message is too religious, too divisive, and too offensive.[77]

But the Church must not allow culture, society, or politics to dictate, bully or influence what it does. Christianity's activities must be guided by the Great Commission and the rest of the New Testament.

---

[76] Matthew 5:13-16

[77] Romans 1:14-16; 1 Corinthians 1:18, 23-25

CHAPTER SEVEN

THE EFFECTS OF POSTMODERNISM ON THE CHURCH - PART TWO

> *The Lord GOD has given Me the tongue of the learned, That I should know how to speak a word in season to him who is weary. He awakens Me morning by morning, He awakens My ear to hear as the learned.*
> *Isaiah 50:4*

Banning "Christianese"

A lady visited one of our weekly Bible Studies a number of years ago. During the Bible Study, I invited the attenders to give testimonies of what God had been doing in their lives that week. Two or three testified by starting out, "I praise God…" or "I thank God…"

At the close of each testimony, others chimed in, "Amen!" and "Praise the Lord!"

Even the children in our church, as young as four or five years old know how to testify and they all start out with, "I praise God for…" or "I thank God because… ."

Finally, this lady opened her testimony like this, "I am confused now, because I came from another church and the pastor over there told us that we are not allowed to say, 'Praise God,' 'Thank God,' 'Thank you,

Jesus,' 'Hallelujah' or things like that anymore because we shouldn't use religious language anymore. That pastor said it is offensive to unbelievers and we should not, under any circumstances, use Christian phrases anymore."

That is just plain Postmodern-laced, contextualized-based, wrong-headed guidance. Only in the Postmodern Era has speaking "Christianese" been blackballed in Christianity.

The world can't get saved if you never use Biblical terms in reaching them. So… we have to explain our terms. So what? Then let's take the time to explain them, because the power to save is in the Gospel message and not in vague and cryptic humanistic garble![78]

I proactively teach our church "Christianese" and encourage them to speak it with confidence. While I'm preaching and teaching, I will freely use Bible words like sanctification, atonement, redemption, propitiation, regeneration, covenant, and vicarious, etc. and explain to the congregation what they mean.

I would rather the people in our church speak Christianese comfortably than be skilled in worldly conversation.

Just Colorful Language?

I cringe whenever I hear ministers in the pulpit carelessly throw around phrases like, "My God" and "Oh my God." Is that just another non-consequential style point too?

True, we live under grace and not under the Mosaic Law but how did violating the Second Commandment[79] become so fashionable for born-again believers and ministers? Using this phrase so loosely in the pulpit can leave the listener with the mistaken notion that it is okay with God to use His name in the same careless way that the world does… as nothing more than an expression. When the world uses phrases like these

---

[78] Romans 1:16; 1 Corinthians 2:4-5

[79] Exodus 20:7

as profanity, the believer would be better off avoiding their use in similar ways.

And, why are believers so comfortable now using such worldly acronym terms as OMG?

It is not enough to defend with, "Well, it is just an expression and, anyway, to me it means 'Oh My Goodness.'"

When we type OMG in our Facebook or Twitter comments, do we really believe that everyone else is reading it as "Oh My Goodness?"

Are all these mere non-substantive "style" points, as well? Really? Have conservative Evangelical, Pentecostal, and Full Gospel standards really slid so far south?

I have a 1970s era button which bears the original acronym from Christianity in the modern times. The button reads,

"Please, BPWMGIFWMY."

Translation:

"Please, be patient with me, God isn't finished with me yet." Now there is a great acronym for the believer!

When I was growing up, h-e-double-toothpick and d*mn were officially considered swear words. Even well into the 1990s these words were not allowed on live TV. Today, however, these words are no longer on the "naughty word list."

Back in the 1970s, my parents were close friends with a young couple who were new believers. Mom and Dad were helping them to grow in their faith. The husband was a farmer. One day, he was trying to repair his busted tractor. He worked for hours to no avail. The longer he worked, the more frustrated and angrier he became, so the old cuss words from his pre-Christ days began to flow.

Over and over, he began to mumble in anger, "God d*mn it." Everything seemed to be going from bad to worse.

Finally, as he started back for the house totally discouraged he prayed, "Lord, why aren't You helping me?"

He told my parents later, "The minute I prayed that to the Lord, the Holy Spirit spoke in my heart and said, 'How can I fix what you keep asking Me to curse?'"

He repented immediately and asked for forgiveness. When he went back out to try again after lunch, he got some fresh ideas on what to look for and do. The tractor got fixed that same day and he learned a valuable life lesson in his young walk with Lord.

Believers do not need substitutes for unchristian language, such as, "h*ck" instead of h-e-double-toothpick. Or "d*rn" instead of "d*mn". Or "shoot" or "cr*p" instead of the s-word.[80]

This manner of speech is not befitting for a Christian!

We need not rely only upon the Old Testament Second Commandment[81] to find out what God thinks of careless words and "colorful language." The New Testament has plenty to say about them too.

Jesus, for example, said in Matthew 12:36,

> **36 But I tell you that men will give an account on the day of judgment for every careless word they have spoken.[82]**

And, in Ephesians 4:29, we read,

> **29 Let no foul or polluting language, nor evil word nor unwholesome or worthless talk [ever] come out of your mouth, but only such [speech] as is good and beneficial to the spiritual progress of others, as is fitting to the need and the occasion, that it may be a blessing and give grace (God's favor) to those who hear it.[83]**

---

[80] Obviously, this author will also use words like s*ck(s), d*mn, h-e-double-toothpick when their original meaning and context are required and applied, but never as swear words or loosely spoken substitutes for swearing.

[81] Exodus 20:7

[82] Berean Study Bible Translation

[83] AMPC Bible

While it is true that all of us, without exception, occasionally say some pretty careless and unwholesome things which hurt instead of edify, we should be able to agree that the easiest way to begin to practice the instruction found in these verses is by ridding ourselves from using the world's cuss list, expressions, their acronyms and substitutes. Words such as: cr*p, h*ck, p*ss, d*rn, and s*cks have no place in the vocabulary and conversation of a saint.

I hardly think that we will be using such language in heaven! Believers, especially ministers, let's clean up our speech![84]

It is time for every believer individually and every local church to take an honest, self-reflecting assessment as to how and why we have come to this point of such loose standards in our traditionally conservative Evangelical / Pentecostal / Full Gospel heritage.[85]

Forgetting: the Spirit of Disloyalty

10 For God is not <u>unrighteous</u> (unjust), <u>so as to forget</u> your work and the love which you showed toward his name, in that you served the saints, and still do serve them.[86]

Another of sad characteristic flourishing in the Postmodern Christianity today is disloyalty.

Disloyalty runs off of dual engines: unrighteousness and forgetfulness.

In the verse above, the Bible tells us that God is not unjust or unrighteous, so as to forget what we have done for Him here on earth. So, what do we take away from this verse?

Unjust and unrighteous character forgets; just and righteous character does not.

Righteousness + Remembering = Loyalty and Honor

Unrighteousness + Forgetting = Disloyalty and Dishonor

---

[84] Titus 2:7-8, Proverbs 17:20

[85] 1 Peter 4:17; 2 Corinthians 13:1,5

[86] Hebrews 6:10 New Heart English Bible (parenthesis and emphasis added)

It's pretty much that simple.

But forget what? The unjust/unrighteous person forgets the grace, blessings, favors, and mercy shown to them. The spirit of disloyalty forgets the good that God, or a person, has done.

The fact that God remembers (i.e.: takes a record of) your service to Him speaks to the righteous and just nature of His character and integrity.[87]

In other words, God doesn't let you go on serving Him and then not give that service due recognition and reward. He doesn't take advantage of you and then drop you like a rock, leaving you empty, which is the way so many behave today.

Unfortunately, the spirit of forgetting runs rampant in the character of *man*, even in born-again believers. When people forget, they become ungrateful and disloyal. Hebrews 6:10 says that this kind of forgetfulness is unrighteous and unjust.

Think about Absalom, the son of David.

Absalom was the third son of David. He had a sister named Tamar who was violated by their half-brother, Amnon. In the course of time, Absalom, took revenge on Amnon and had him killed. Absalom ran away to hide from justice.

Eventually, David's servant, Joab, is sent to recall Absalom to Jerusalem. He is told not to leave the city and that he will not be allowed to see the king… but, he will be spared from the death penalty for killing Amnon.

That all worked for a while. Absalom was back in Jerusalem, and it seemed that the matter had fallen by the wayside.

Then, in that comfort zone, Absalom began to forget. He forgot that he murdered his half-brother, Amnon. He forgot that his father, David, had shown him mercy by allowing him to come back to Jerusalem to live and by sparing him from facing the death penalty.

---

[87] Romans 2:5-9; 2 Corinthians 5:10

Because Absalom was an ***unrighteous*** man, he ***forgot***, and he became ***disloyal*** to his own father. There was not a loyal bone in his body. He paid back the mercy he had received from his father by staging a coup d'état against his own father which even yielded temporary success.

The whole story is found in Second Samuel chapters 13-18.

This "forgetting" and the disloyalty it produces is a big problem in Postmodern Christianity, especially in ministry and church life. Think of how many churches have been torn apart by church splits because of the spirit of forgetting and disloyalty at work. That is the spirit of Absalom.

During our ministry years in the Philippines, God used my parents and me to give a lot of people, Filipinos and Americans, their start in the ministry. We were happy that this was one way God was using us in missions ministry.

There was one young woman who graduated from the same Bible School that I graduated from in the U.S. who got her start in missions ministry through us. She graduated about nine or ten years behind me. I happened to meet her while visiting in the U.S. She felt called of God to minister in the Philippines but had nowhere to start. We invited her to come and help in our Bible School. God used the Cedergrens to give her, her start.

She gained experience, stature, and made lots and lots of contacts for herself while teaching in our Bible School. She met the man who later became her husband there. He was a student in the school and they got together after his graduation. She built up her own base by tapping all the resources available to her through her connection to our ministry.

Eventually, she and her husband went off to build their own Bible School, staffing it completely with graduates from our school. We were happy for them and continued to give them encouragement and legal covering for their ministry until they were able to legally establish their own ministry.

And then one day, a few years later, when some rogue graduates (with their own story of forgetting and disloyalty) made big trouble for our Bible School, this lady and her husband allied with the rogue graduates. The head troublemaker was actually an enemy of theirs until he became an enemy of the Cedergrens, then this disloyal couple switched sides. Instead of standing with the people and ministry which had helped them build their family and ministry, they stood with the rebellious troublemakers.

They had convinced themselves by that time, several years on, that they got where they were in life and ministry on their own, by themselves. They forgot who God had used to give them a place to start in missions and help build up their own ministry.

Forgetting something that important is unrighteous. It is the spirit of disloyalty at work.

By contrast, I will forever remember and honor the man God used in my life to give me my first chance in missions, at the age of 19, when no one else would, the late Brother (Virgle J.) Howell.

Bro. Howell ordained me into the ministry in the Philippines on my 23rd birthday. I have not forgotten how the Lord used him in my life, nor will I ever forget. I have kept honor for him in my heart all these years. I would never join or side with anyone who would dishonor Bro. Howell or oppose him, not during his life nor via the ministry he founded. The ministry he founded has blessed me with friendship and legal covering in America since I first met Bro. Howell in 1980, continuing to this very day.

That is the spirit of loyalty, because, to borrow from the phrasing found in Hebrews 6:10:

I am not unrighteous (unjust) so as to forget Bro. Howell's labor of love as he (unknowingly) mentored my ministerial life in Jesus' name.

The Bible says in Proverbs 30:11 (TLB),

> *11 There is a kind of person who curses his father and does not bless his mother.*

The child (natural, figurative, or spiritual) who forgets (does not honor) in adulthood all the sacrifices and good the parents did for them in their youth is a living example of the spirit of disloyalty.

So much unrighteous forgetting (i.e.: disloyalty) is happening throughout humanity today and in the Church.

Pastors will be the first to admit that they are not perfect but it is crazy tough for pastors today. It could be said of pastors that they are gluttons for punishment. They invest a lot of heart, prayer, time, and emotion directly into the lives of the people in their congregations.

One of the most heartbreaking parts of pastoring is when people leave the church, especially those who had received so much from, and been so long in, the church. To see the very people they watched grow up, helped, taught, counselled at all hours of the day or night, ministered to, water baptized, prayed over, stood alongside with in times of great need, gave opportunities to serve to, trained, and mentored, etc., so quickly and easily dump both pastor and church when it suits their pride and flesh is beyond painful for pastors.

There is blame to be shared for this unrighteous trend in the Church and ministry today. Postmodern culture and philosophy play a huge role. The "self-made" nature of the Postmodern generation through social media and YouTube are contributors to the high level of betrayal and disloyalty in our society today. People convince themselves that they are self-made, spiritual Christians as they pick and choose only "feel-good" messages on YouTube that tickle their ears. They forget how God used their pastor to help them grow. In their purview, it is the pastor and local church who owe them something for coming.

Some responsibility also rests on pastors and ministers who fail morally or focus more on building their own fame and ministry kingdom than on faithfully and humbly caring for the sheep.

Is it any wonder the divorce rate and the prevailing sentiment to live together in uncommitted relationships rather than get married is so high?

Too many people do not want to commit, and those who do get married all too often forget as the years roll on. This is the spirit of disloyalty at work in society today.

In the Book of Psalms, David reveals the anguish he felt as he suffered betrayal and disloyalty... not from an enemy, but from someone who had been his friend.[88]

Even Jesus lost some disciples in John 6:60-69. Thankfully, none from among the twelve disciples walked away.

> *66 As a result of this <u>many of His disciples left, and would no longer walk with Him.</u> 67 So Jesus said to the twelve, "You do not want to leave also, do you?" 68 Simon Peter answered Him, "Lord, to whom shall we go? You have words of eternal life. 69 And we have already believed and have come to know that You are the Holy One of God. (emphasis added)*

May each of us forever come to the same conclusion regarding our own commitment to Jesus that Disciple Peter, gave above.

One day some time ago, out of the blue, I received a book in our church mailbox entitled, *Loyalty and Disloyalty: Those Who Forget.*[89] The author lists ten people that we should never forget and always hold with honor in our hearts:

1. The person who led you to Christ.
2. The person who taught you the fundamentals of your Christian faith.
3. The person who inspired you to go into the ministry.
4. The person who taught you how to preach.
5. The person who taught you about life.

---

[88] Psalm 55:12-14
[89] ©2011 Deg Heward-Mills, page 79

6. The person who trained you in the ministry.
7. The person who gave you an opportunity in ministry.
8. The person who loved you and had faith in you.
9. The person who goes ahead of you and fights for you.
10. The person who helped you financially.

Many of the foregoing points speak of the people God uses in the lives of young ministers who are just getting started in the ministry. Other points also describe the role of the pastor in the local church. Something to think about, isn't it?

Pray for your pastor and home church regularly and develop an attitude of gratitude for your church family. Be forbearing and forgiving, submitted and involved, committed and loyal to your home church just as others in the church family are towards you.[90]

This is how you can guard against the spirit of forgetting and disloyalty.

Divorce is a Blessing?

Sad to say, news of scandal, apostasy, ministers slipping into false doctrines,[91] and the moral, ethical, and financial failure among pastors and leaders of ministry, both great and small, are no longer much of a surprise in the Modern-Postmodern eras. This trend began its uptick in earnest back in the mid-1980s when the financial and moral scandals of two or three high profile televangelists broke and became public. Loss of faith (apostasy), doctrinal failure, and scandal among ministers have been on the rise ever since.

Moral failure and scandals have far-reaching consequences, and not just for the people they happen to. For example, unsaved people use the scandalous behavior of Christian ministers as an excuse not to receive Christ. Weak believers often stumble and backslide as the preachers

---

[90] I Corinthians 16:15-18; Galatians 6:6; 1 Thessalonians 5:12-13; Hebrews 13:17
[91] 1 Timothy 4:1

they had respected fall from grace. And, the Gospel and reputation of all Christian ministry suffers humiliation with each new black eye.[92]

I have heard divorced and remarried ministers testify that they are so thankful to God for their divorce. They reason out that only now can they finally truly relate to members in their congregation who are facing divorce too.

Only a minister who has been through divorce can effectively empathize with and counsel a church member going through one, they say. Nonsense.

I was shocked several years ago when I heard a someone make the following remark, "Brother (Kenneth E.) Hagin would not be very effective in ministry if he were still alive today because the Church has moved on and his style of preaching just wouldn't be effective."

Not only is that a sad comment. It also happens to be untrue.

The trend today seems to be that the dirtier, more foul or fallen the past or current life of the minister, the more worldly their speech, dress and appearance... the more they are deemed equipped to reach this generation because they can "relate" to the debased condition of the unsaved through their own personal experience in ways that a believer with a clean past and a good testimony cannot. This line of reasoning argues that every sinful, fallen experience the minister undergoes actually works to make them a far cooler and more relatable minister of God.

How completely false that is! That would make Jesus the most unqualified and ineffective minister, counselor, and evangelist ever, since the Bible makes it quite clear that He never sinned.[93]

In the early 1960s, David Wilkerson started a ministry to gangs in New York City which eventually spread worldwide. Teen Challenge has been instrumental in bringing the Gospel to inner city streets all over

---

[92] Matthew 18:6-10; Romans 14:13; 1 Corinthians 8:9; 2 Corinthians 6:3; 1 John 2:10
[93] 2 Corinthians 5:21; 1 Peter 2:22; Hebrews 4:15; 1 John 3:5

the world. In 1970, a movie entitled, *The Cross and the Switchblade*, was released to tell his story. That movie and David Wilkerson's story had a great impact on my life. What has stayed with me from it is *how* David reached out with the Gospel to the gangs on the streets of New York. He went dressed in his pastor's suitcoat and tie. He did not shed himself of or hide his identity as a small church pastor. He showed them genuine care and offered them a straightforward Gospel message. He did not change his clothing style to match theirs, did not exchange his suit and tie for black leathers and chains. He did not grow his hair out to match their hair styles or fill his body with tattoos, yet his sincere approach resulted in hundreds of lives being won for Christ and receiving freedom from drugs and gang violence then, and tens of thousands more worldwide over the years since. David Wilkerson did not believe that he needed to look and talk like the people he was trying to reach.

Ministers are not to preach, teach and counsel from their own weaknesses. We are called to minister from the authority of God's Word, grace, anointing and Calling with all humility. In the end what counts is what God's Word says about a matter. Period.

Always remember this, dear Reader:

The devil is devoid of loyalty. First, he will entrap the minister (or believer) in sin. Then the accuser of the brethren[94] will make good use of the scandal through public exposure, causing shame and disgrace to the minister, and subsequently tarnishing the cause of Christ in the process.[95]

Sure, God's Word clearly offers restoration for anyone who seeks forgiveness regardless of how serious their moral failures were, however, why is it that the Church seems keener on making heroes and stars out of fallen ministers than on calling both minister and disciple to humble, holy living in the first place?

---

[94] Revelation 12:10

[95] 2 Corinthians 6:3

Are these really to be the new qualifications that one must have on their ministerial resumé to be thought of as effective and successful in the ministry today? Emergent/Emerging-influenced Christianity seems to believe so:

Have the testimony of a ruined past. Live an "alternative lifestyle" (or at least accept such lifestyles). Be divorced (whether before salvation or, better yet, as a minister). Have a "Christian" tattoo (the more the better). Never speak "Christianese." Avoid using the Name of Jesus. Preach about self-help, politics, and social issues and do not draw from the Bible too much. Use Star Wars or Harry Potter characters for sermon illustrations and elevate their greatness instead of using Biblical characters or the lives of brave heroes from church history. Emphasize feelings over truth. Emphasize a social justice message over repentance from sin. And for goodness' sake, do not call believers to holy living because that is Premodern and old-fashioned legalism. Plus, in doing so, you might offend someone!

How do you spell "sin"?

The Bible teaches us that "accepting Christ," "being saved," "becoming born-again" means more than just securing a ticket into heaven for when we die. Truly following Christ involves complete life and lifestyle transformation.[96] But because of Postmodern cancel culture inside the Church, the whole Biblical position on sin has largely been "cancelled."

Sadly, in many of today's churches, there is precious little preaching about turning away from sin and sinful lifestyles. Doing so is regarded as out-of-touch, judgmental, and offensive in today's Postmodern environment. Postmodern churches prefer to feed their sheep feel-good topics on self-help, being a good person, and the "inner goodness" in

---

[96] 2 Corinthians 5:17; 2 Peter 1:3-4

the heart of *man*, all topics which run contrary to what God's Word says about the unregenerate heart.[97]

However, believe it or not, it is possible for a pastor to preach on sin without the message being filled with condemnation, and if the message does result repentance and turnaround in the life of a listener because of godly conviction, then we say, "Hallelujah!"

Again, it is absolutely possible to preach on holiness without the message being filled with a spirit of stifling legalism.

Too often, pastors swayed by Postmodern culture become afraid to teach publicly or counsel privately that living together outside the bond of marriage is sin. But why are they afraid? Mostly because they are afraid of offending, and subsequently losing, people from their church, so they whisper to the couple, "Just don't be too public about your lifestyle here in the church."

With a wink of the eye, aberrant lifestyles, alcohol, smoking, drugs, worldly dancing, gambling, cursing, wife and child abuse, etc. are now being tolerated or left unconfronted and uncounseled in some Evangelical and Pentecostal churches.[98] This trend is happening all over the world now in the streams of Christianity which had been historically reliable for standing by the standards of godly living found in God's Word.

The Church has been losing ground to Postmodernism for a long time now on important moral issues because its embrace of contextualization early on required compromise.

Europe, for example, fell to Postmodernism and became Post-Christian several decades ago. America is about 30-40 years behind Europe in caving to Postmodern philosophy and becoming post-Christian.

Remember what Postmodernism is all about: no absolutes, no fixed, inviolable truth, consequently... right and wrong are a matter of one's

---

[97] Jeremiah 17:9; Mark 7:21-23
[98] Leviticus 10:10; Ezekiel 22:26; Ezekiel 44:23

own personal interpretation. This is exactly the mindset of the average European. Most Europeans have no idea what sin is or what the word even means.

Sadly, America is racing speedily down that same road.

Salvation, on the other hand, fundamentally requires that a person acknowledge their need to be saved from that which they cannot save themselves![99]

Try explaining the need for God's forgiveness and salvation to a post-Christian European and they will likely laugh in your face.

"I don't need God. I am a good person. There is nothing I need to be saved from. Sin? What is that? I don't believe in the afterlife anyway," are likely replies.

Many years ago, a married couple came to me. The Filipina wife was a believer, but the European husband was not saved. He had questions about Christianity.

First, he explained his opinion about what makes a person right with God. It was the standard humanistic spiel about being good and that it doesn't matter which religion people believe in because, in the end, all religions believe in the same God (god) etc., etc. So, I opened the Bible in front of him and read a few verses, such as, John 14:6, Acts 4:12, and 1 Timothy 2:5.

To that he indignantly replied, "Jesus can't be the only way to heaven. What about all the people who don't believe in Jesus? What will happen to them?"

The Holy Spirit quickened me to reply that ultimately they will stand before God and be judged by their works.

He was glad to hear that and said, "Ah, that's good then. They still have a chance."

I countered with, "No, that's bad."

---

[99] Ephesians 2:8-9

And then I went on to show him from Isaiah 64:6, Romans 3:10-11 and Revelation 20:11-15 that everyone who is depending on getting into heaven by their good works (self-goodness) is going to end up in the lake of fire instead.

"No," replied this Post-Christian European, "I cannot accept this."

Sadly, until this very day, he still hasn't.

It is probably easier to win someone to Christ who grew up under Islam, atheism or Communism than it is to win a Post-Christian, Postmodern Westerner.

The Post-Christian, Postmodern Western world has become one of the neediest harvest fields in our world today.[100]

The Bottom Line

Many conservative Evangelical and Full Gospel Christians in America are horrified by what they see as the effects of liberal politics, "Cancel Culture," and "Wokeism" on American society... The attack on free speech, gun rights and American history and culture, political correctness, the war on Christmas, abortion, transgender men taking over in women's sports and beauty pageants, and other perversions of every kind.

Sad to say, Postmodern America is also going Post-Christian at breakneck speed.

I am also grieved by these very evil Postmodern trends in society, culture and politics. These are taking our world into a very dark place today to be sure.

However, what should concern every lover of Jesus Christ far more is the spiritual and morally degraded condition of the Church and the fact that Western Christianity has been practicing its own inhouse brand of "Cancel Biblical Culture" for well over thirty years now through contextualization.[101]

Lord, have mercy.

---

[100] Matthew 9:36-38; John 4:35
[101] 1 Peter 4:15-17

CHAPTER EIGHT

LESSONS FROM MARS HILL

> **"**
>
> And *my message and my preaching were not in persuasive words of wisdom, but in demonstration of the Spirit and of power,* 5 so that your faith would not rest on the wisdom of men, but on the power of God..
>
> *1 Corinthians 2:4-5 (emphasis added)*

Jesus Ate and Drank with Sinners

There are two main accounts in the New Testament that Postmodern Christians like to run to in defending their culture-contextualized version of Christianity.

First, they are quick to refer to verses that talk about Jesus "eating and drinking with sinners" and that He was called a "friend of sinners."[102]

Invoking the "Jesus ate and drank with sinners" verses is a well-worn argument some Christians go to for cover over their own inner desire to do the same things the unsaved are doing like living in various kinds of immoral and perverse lifestyles, drinking, partying, etc. and still feel okay about it.

---

[102] Matthew 9:10-13; 11:19; Mark 2:15-17; Luke 5:29-32; 7:34

Jesus was indeed a "friend to sinners" in the sense that He cared about them, showed mercy, and offered forgiveness to any sinner who humbly came to Him, but He neither condoned nor participated in their sinfulness in His role as "a friend to sinners."

Several years ago, when American Evangelical and Pentecostal/Full Gospel Christianity was still known for its conservative values, I spent about 10-12 weeks in the northern middle part of England. I went there to help a small Full Gospel church on a ministerial level. The first evening I arrived, the lady who hosted me in her home during my stay gave a dinner in honor of my arrival. After the meal prayer, she stood up, got a bottle of wine, and began to serve everyone.

When she came to me, I politely said, "May I have a glass of water, please?"

With that, she lit into quite a tirade against me,

"Oh, I know you are an American Christian, and they don't drink. But you know, Jesus turned the water into wine and Paul told Timothy to drink wine for the sake of his health. It is not wrong for Christians to drink alcohol. The New Testament does not forbid the Christian from drinking alcohol. We are free in Christ. We live in the world too. God understands, etc."

On and on she went for several moments. I did not interrupt her but waited patiently for her to finish. When she finally did take a breath, I just looked up and politely repeated my request for a glass of water. Since she did not have a debate partner in me,[103] the subject ended awkwardly and abruptly, and we continued on with our dinner.

About a week later, the church announced that they would do what they called a "soft evangelism" event on the following Saturday night. Boy oh boy oh boy, was it ever "soft!" It turned out to be so "soft" that the event had no spiritual value or substance for Christ at all!

---

[103] Proverbs 15:3

They rented a small pub-like town hall establishment and advertised that there would be a talent show held there, sponsored by this church. On the flyer, they wrote that people should come and present their talent of any kind and that it would be a BYOB evening. BYOB means "Bring Your Own Bottle" (of alcohol). The church members showed up with bottles of various kinds of alcohol, sang worldly songs, read philosophical, worldly poems, and told worldly jokes the whole evening! They were as drunk as the unbelievers sitting next to them. Not even one believer from the church put forth a clear presentation of the Gospel because everyone was too drunk! I was literally the only person in that gathering of about 40-50 adults, roughly equally mixed between church members and unsaved, who did not drink anything. I sat there absolutely fuming on the inside. I could hardly stand to remain in the building. When one of the leaders from the church noticed how unhappy I was, she told me that this was their way of proving to unbelievers that they were not judgmental, "holier-than-thou" Christians. They justified this method of "soft evangelism" with the Scripture verses about Jesus eating and drinking with sinners. Wow! Not one single unbeliever came even a millimeter closer to getting saved that night. There was absolutely no impact for heaven or eternity. All that happened as a result of that night of debauchery was that the next morning, the church members were largely subdued during praise and worship because so many of them were suffering from hangovers. Even those who led worship were drunk the night before but playing music and leading praise and worship the next morning in church.

I can't think of a more blatant example of failed results when Christians try to impress the world through contextualization! Those believers had convinced themselves that there was no inconsistency with their being worldly and getting drunk on Saturday night and then praising God on Sunday morning.

In my first year of living in Switzerland, I was invited to a wedding reception. A minister from the Swiss Reformed Protestant Church was also invited and was seated next to me at the table. The man was Scottish and had lived in Switzerland for a number of years. As we were exchanging pleasantries, the wedding host gave the Reformed minister a glass of wine, asking him to taste the wine before it was to be served to everyone. Asking him to do this was a gesture of high honor to him for his presence at the feast. He swirled the glass like a pro, smelled and tasted the wine, and finished off with profuse compliments for their choice. Smiling proudly, the host began to serve each guest. When he came to me, I politely requested water. With that, the Reformed minister echoed the same tune I had heard years earlier at the Full Gospel church in northern England,

"Oh, I see that you are an American Christian and American Christians don't drink alcohol. Well, you know, Jesus turned the water into wine and ate and drank with sinners, so I figure it's not a problem. I'm from Scotland and before I came to Switzerland, I also didn't drink but I learned to drink over the years that I've lived here because that is what the locals do. You will learn to drink too, just wait..."

Well, I never did learn to drink alcohol in all the years I've lived in Europe because neither geography nor environment determine my values. My faith and convictions come from God's Word, and these are what I live by. I have the same faith and convictions regardless of where I live or who I am with.

It used to be that being born-again automatically came with the understanding that you stopped doing the "vices" like drinking alcohol and smoking, partying, worldly dancing, gambling, cursing, etc...

Unfortunately, many Evangelical and Full Gospel Christians from even such historically conservative places like the U.S. and the Philippines are now also dancing to the beat of the Postmodern, contextualized drums today. That dance is no longer just for nominal, mainline, denominational Christianity anymore, as it once had been.

A few years ago, I sat down for lunch with three other Full Gospel ministers in Europe. We were on a lunch break during a day of teaching in a Bible School. They all belonged to the same ministerial association. As is often the custom in many European restaurants, there was an unopened bottle of wine on the table which sparked a short conversation like this:

Minister A playfully asked, "Anyone want a glass of wine with lunch?"

Minister B answered, "I would but we really aren't supposed to drink in our ministerial organization. Do you guys drink?"

Minister A replied, "I asked the head of our ministerial organization if it was really wrong for us to drink a simple glass of wine with a meal since it is a very European thing to do. The head of the organization whispered to me that he won't hold it against me if I do it quietly because he understands that it is part of European culture. He told me just not do it when we are at our organization's conferences and big meetings. He told me to keep it under the radar," and then turning to the waitress, he said, "I would like to order a glass of wine, please."

I was not surprised anymore because I had been living in Europe for several years at that point, but sad to say, so many in Christianity are fast adapting the ways of the unsaved world and overriding conscience to feel okay about it. It is not just a post-Christian European thing anymore. Historically conservative Evangelical and Full Gospel Christians everywhere are now taking their liberties in nearly every facet of moral life and conduct.

The second problem with the whispered advice of the head of the ministerial organization is that it gave the "all clear" for hypocrisy. It was a soft endorsement that leading a double life is acceptable for ministers as long as the hidden part isn't "too bad" or sinful in excess.

There used to be noticeably clear "red lines" that Evangelical and Full Gospel believers and ministers did not cross. In Postmodern Christianity, however, almost every area of moral life and standards have now turned gray. Red lines that had historically guided Evangelical and Full Gospel Christian values and standards for centuries are now blurred or disappearing altogether in this environment of Postmodern Christianity... all in the name of packaging and getting along with modern culture.

In the end, the question is not whether or not engaging in these types of "worldly vices" affects one's salvation, or whether or not the Bible allows Christians to drink. No, the real issue is the believer's testimony before the world.

The Bible clearly teaches us that in our evangelistic approach, we must encourage the unsaved to come to Christ "just as they are." This is the Good News, that He welcomes them just as they are. *Just as I am without one plea.*[104]

All that is fine and good and correct, but it is *our* testimony before the unsaved world that I am talking about, not what they need to do to get saved.

If the way the Christian lives is no different than the world, what would compel the world to receive our Gospel?[105]

Are we really to offer a Gospel which simply turns a violent, depressed unsaved drunk into a happy alcoholic in Christ?

What message are we communicating to the world when we work so hard at making them feel comfortable about bringing the sins of their ruined past into the faith we are offering them?[106]

> *1 Christ suffered while he was in his body. So you should strengthen yourselves with the same kind of thinking Christ had. The one who accepts suffering in this life has clearly decided to <u>stop sinning</u>. 2 Strengthen yourselves so that you will live your lives here on earth doing what God wants, not the evil things that people want to do. 3 <u>In the past</u> you wasted too much time doing what those who don't know God like to do. You <u>were</u> living immoral lives, doing the evil*

---

[104] Words by Charlotte Elliott (1789-1871); Music by William B. Bradbury (1816-1868)
[105] Galatians 2:14
[106] Romans 6:11-19; 13:11-14; 14:16-22; Galatians 2:14

things you wanted to do. You <u>were</u> always getting drunk, having wild drinking parties, and doing shameful things in your worship of idols. 4 Now those "friends" think it is strange that you <u>no longer</u> join them in all the wild and wasteful things they do. And so they say bad things about you.[107]

In the 1970s, my dad led a young musician from our home town to Christ. John Peterson was one of the most gifted guitar and banjo players that ever came out of Minnesota. He was a country western music guy who had played and sung back-up in the bands of famous country music artists in Nashville and Memphis before he decided to move back home to Minnesota.

Salvation took hold in John and produced complete life transformation. John wanted to serve God from day one, but he still had almost a year's contract left with the country western band he was playing with in bars and nightclubs across Minnesota and Wisconsin. So, John began to add the song, *Amazing Grace*, at the end of every song set before he would go on break. He never touched another drop of alcohol after he got born-again.

During his breaks and at the end of each show, he would sit down with people in the bar and tell them about Christ. He prayed with many people to receive Christ in the ensuing months.

Finally, about 8-9 months of evangelizing this way, he got discouraged and asked the Lord, "Lord, why are all the people who I have prayed with to accept You still sitting here every Friday and Saturday night? Why isn't there any change in their lives? Why are they still here in the bar?"

---

[107] 1 Peter 4:1-4 ERV (emphasis added)

Just like that, the Holy Spirit answered John in his spirit, "Well, you are still here too, aren't you?"

John repented, broke his contract, and laid down his guitar with firm resolve to never play guitar or banjo again.

About three months had passed when he told this story to my dad. Praise God, my dad was able to explain to John that he didn't need to stop playing guitar and banjo, but that he should start using his God-given gift of music in a better way.

From that day on until he went home to be with the Lord in 1999, God used the life of John Peterson to reach thousands and thousands of people for Christ through his music and evangelistic ministry. God gave him a very fruitful ministry with young people as he led hundreds to the Lord and then mentored most of them in their new Christian faith.

In the Bible books of Romans, Galatians and First Corinthians, Paul wrote that just because we have spiritual freedom in Christ does not mean that we should use that liberty as a license to satisfy sinful, worldly desires.[108]

The Mars Hill Flop

The second place in Scripture that Postmodern Christians will run to in trying to make their case for reshaping Christianity at every level [the church sanctuary, church services, church life, standards for believers, etc.] into that which is as fashionable and attractive to the Millennial generation as possible is the Apostle Paul's sermon on Mars Hill.

For many Christians, Paul's sermon on Mars Hill is the perfect justification for contextualizing the Gospel. Allow me to set up the scene:

Paul was the first one to preach the Gospel on the European continent. As he left Troas, which is on the northwestern-most tip of modern-day Turkey, he sailed to the Greek Macedonian city of Neapolis (modern-day

---

[108] Romans Chapter 6; Galatians Chapter 5; 1 Corinthians 6:12; 10:23; 1 Peter 2:16

Kavala), and from there he traveled inland to the city of Philippi. Acts 16:12 tells us that Philippi was a prominent city in Macedonia. On their first Sabbath in Philippi, Paul and his companions went to the riverside to find a place to pray. They found some women there and shared the Gospel with them. These women were the first on the European continent to believe the Gospel message and were baptized in the nearby river.[109]

Paul's ministry in Philippi was significant. It was there that he cast the spirit of divination out of a slave girl. That good deed landed Paul and Silas in prison after being severely beaten. The Bible says in Acts 16:25 that Paul and Silas prayed and sang hymns in their prison cell so loudly that the other prisoners heard them. God caused an earthquake to rattle the jail and their chains were loosed. Long story short, they led the jailor to Christ. Paul preached to the jailor's whole household, and they believed and were water baptized.[110]

From Philippi, Paul traveled to the city of Thessalonica where he also had much success in winning souls and planting a church. His method of ministry? A straightforward presentation of the Gospel as he had done everywhere he went, declaring the death, burial, and resurrection of Jesus Christ.[111]

From Thessalonica, Paul travelled further inland to the Macedonian city of Berea. Acts 17:11 says that the Bereans were much more noble than the Thessalonians as they "searched the Scriptures" diligently to see if the things Paul was preaching were true.

Eventually, Paul made his way southward to Athens. As was his custom in every place, he went to the local Jewish synagogue first and then to the local marketplace.[112] The philosophers that heard him speak brought him to Mars Hill in Athens where Paul gave his famous

---

[109] Acts 16:13-15
[110] Acts 16:25-34
[111] 1 Thessalonians 1:5
[112] Acts 17:17

sermon. Mars Hill was the place where people from all over the world came to when in Athens to share their ideas, beliefs, and philosophies. In London's Hyde Park there is a similar kind of place called "Speaker's Corner" where anyone can stand and tell, preach or vent their ideas and views. Traditionally, it is a bastion of free speech. Mars Hill in Athens was such a place in Paul's day.

Some theologians claim that this was Paul's greatest sermon. Others say it was his worst. Here is the full text of his sermon from Acts chapter seventeen:

> *22 So Paul stood in the midst of the Areopagus and said, 'Men of Athens, I observe that you are very religious in all respects. 23 For while I was passing through and examining the objects of your worship, I also found an altar with this inscription, 'TO AN UNKNOWN GOD.' Therefore what you worship in ignorance, this I proclaim to you. 24 The God who made the world and all things in it, since He is Lord of heaven and earth, does not dwell in temples made with hands; 25 nor is He served by human hands, as though He needed anything, since He Himself gives to all people life and breath and all things; 26 and He made from one man every nation of mankind to live on all the face of the earth, having determined their appointed times and the boundaries of their habitation, 27 that they would seek God, if perhaps they might grope for Him and find Him, though He is not far from each one of us; 28 for in Him we live and move and exist, as even some of your own poets have said, 'For we also are His children.' 29 Being then the children of God, we ought not to think that the Divine Nature is like gold or silver or stone, an image formed by the art and thought of man. 30 Therefore having overlooked the times of ignorance, God is now declaring to men that all*

people everywhere should repent, 31 because He has fixed a day in which He will judge the world in righteousness through a Man whom He has appointed, having furnished proof to all men by raising Him from the dead.'

32 Now when they heard of the resurrection of the dead, some began to sneer, but others said, 'We shall hear you again concerning this.' 33 So Paul went out of their midst. 34 But some men joined him and believed, among whom also were Dionysius the Areopagite and a woman named Damaris and others with them.[113]

Although everything he said in this message was true, this was the only time in his illustrious missionary career that Paul tried to contextualize the Gospel to accommodate the philosophies of the local culture, and it flopped… big time!

Paul worked hard for the cause and reputation of the Gospel. Throughout his missionary journeys, he had faithfully preached Jesus as the Messiah. He faithfully preached the death, burial, and resurrection of Jesus Christ. In Romans 1:16, he wrote that the Gospel is the "power of God unto (or, producing) salvation."

In the region of Galatia, Asia Minor, he preached Christ and churches were planted everywhere he went. He preached Christ in Philippi, Thessalonica, and Berea resulting in church plants in each of these cities.

But in Athens, he attempted to contextualize his message to cater to the philosophers of Athens, intentionally omitting the Name of Jesus, and it flopped. Contextualization did not produce any meaningful results for the cause of Christ in Athens.

---

[113] Acts 17:22-34 (emphasis added)

How do we know that it flopped? Because the Bible says that after he finished his message only "some" men believed. The King James translation says, "certain" men believed and joined Paul. The idea behind this word in the Greek is that just a few men believed Paul's message. This is hardly equal to the results he had in Galatia, Ephesus, Macedonia, and other places.

After the Mars Hill flop, Paul left Athens and traveled about fifty-one miles (82 kilometers) west to the city of Corinth. He had learned his lesson in Athens and was determined never to repeat it again.

He went back to preaching a straightforward Gospel in Corinth and the results started piling up once again as they had everywhere Paul preached that Gospel with no compromise! As a result, a thriving church was planted in Corinth. He later wrote to the church in Corinth about the lesson that he had learned in Athens,

> *1 And when I came to you, brethren, I did not come with superiority of speech or of wisdom, proclaiming to you the testimony of God. 2 For I determined to know nothing among you except Jesus Christ, and Him crucified. 3 I was with you in weakness and in fear and in much trembling, 4 and my message and my preaching were not in persuasive words of wisdom, but in demonstration of the Spirit and of power, 5 so that your faith would not rest on the wisdom of men, but on the power of God.* [114]

Paul clearly had the Mars Hill flop in mind, not only when he went to Corinth but also when he wrote these words back to the Corinthian church some years later. You can sense the disdain he had for himself, giving himself a verbal flogging, for trying to win the Athenians by

---

[114] 1 Corinthians 2:1-5

attempting to package the Gospel message in the style, culture, and Athenian philosophy rather than with the Name of Christ.

Although Paul's influence may have eventually contributed to the planting of a church in Athens at some later date, there is no mention in either the New Testament or from early church history that his time there as recorded in Acts directly resulted in a church being planted.

The missionary work of the Apostle Paul in Greece resulted in church plants in Philippi, Thessalonica, Berea (according to established early church history), and Corinth... but not Athens! There is no Pauline "Epistle to the Church at Athens."

Brother (Kenneth E.) Hagin used to say, paraphrasing him, "You don't have to look like the world, talk like the world, dress like the world, and act like the world in order to win the world for Christ. What you need is the anointing of the Holy Spirit and the Gospel. The power to save is in the Gospel."

That power which saves is not found in compromise and the contextualization and adaptation of the Gospel to its surrounding cultural landscape but rather in the faithful and straightforward delivery of the message itself! Just ask DL Moody, John Wesley, Billy Graham, David Wilkerson, Reinhard Bonnke, and others who, collectively, have reached hundreds of millions of souls for heaven, all with a straightforward, no nonsense Gospel message.

When the Church caves to Postmodern culture and its norms, it becomes less effective, not more effective, in delivering to the world around us the Good News message the world so desperately needs.[115]

The Postmodern Church today is doing way too much looking, talking and acting like the world, when we should be looking, talking, and acting like Christ instead!

---

[115] Romans 1:14-16

Chapter Nine

THE EFFECTS OF POSTMODERNISM ON THE CHURCH - PART THREE

> *And as they were burying a man, behold, they saw a marauding band; and they threw the man into the grave of Elisha. And when the man touched the bones of Elisha he revived and stood up on his feet.*
> *2 Kings 13:21*

Without a doubt, the Bible is filled with some really amazing stories. From Genesis to Revelation, we see the involvement of the supernatural in the lives of natural *man*.

Whereas Modernism did its best to indoctrinate *man* into denying the existence of the supernatural realm altogether, Postmodern philosophy almost welcomes the involvement of some aspects of the supernatural in the affairs of *man*. The impact that Postmodern acceptance and inclusion of paranormal activities has had on Christianity is real and significant.

The word *paranormal* means,

> **Beyond the range of normal experience or scientific explanation; Designating or of psychic, occult, supernatural, or other phenomena considered unexplainable by the known forces or laws of nature.** [116]

---

[116] yourdictionary.com/paranormal

Consider these verses which reveal what God thinks about His ministers and His children embracing ideas and idols from the world around them.

> *13 Saul died because he was unfaithful to the LORD; he did not keep the word of the LORD and even consulted a medium for guidance. 1 Chronicles 10:13 NIV*

> *31 Do not turn to mediums or seek out spiritists, for you will be defiled by them. I am the LORD your God. Leviticus 19:31 NIV*

> *6 I will set my face against anyone who turns to mediums and spiritists to prostitute themselves by following them, and I will cut them off from their people. Leviticus 20:6 NIV*

> *19 When someone tells you to consult mediums and spiritists, who whisper and mutter, should not a people inquire of their God? Why consult the dead on behalf of the living? 20 Consult God's instruction and the testimony of warning. If anyone does not speak according to this word, they have no light of dawn. Isaiah 8:19-20 NIV*

Even in the New Testament, under grace, those who have accepted Christ are not to engage in magic and occultism. Even under grace, this is an abomination to the Lord.

> *17 This became known to all, both Jews and Greeks, who lived in Ephesus; and fear fell upon them all and the name of the Lord Jesus was being magnified. 18 Many also of those who had believed kept coming, confessing and disclosing their practices. 19 And many of those who practiced magic*

brought their books together and began burning them in the sight of everyone; and they counted up the price of them and found it fifty thousand pieces of silver. 20 So the word of the Lord was growing mightily and prevailing.[117]

The Bible warns us against participating in all forms of paranormal activities, yet sadly, a large swath of Christianity today seems not to be troubled over assimilating paranormal activities into the Christian experience.

I am not out to name names in this book. That is not my purpose. It is easy enough to do your own research. My purpose here is to call out the activity and sound the alarm, not to name the names either of ministers or church ministries which are possibly involved in or promoting these activities.

The following is only a small sampling of the many perverse ways that Eastern religion, occultism, and the paranormal have infiltrated Postmodern Christianity.

Grave Sucking / Grave Soaking / Mantle Grabbing

In this unscriptural practice, the believer is supposed to find the grave of a famous preacher, pastor or minister and then lay on top of the grave. The belief is that by laying on top of the grave of the departed minister, the believer will receive the same anointing or take onto themselves the very same spiritual mantle that the late man or woman of God had.

This is so ridiculous on its face; it is difficult to grasp how any serious believer in Jesus Christ could engage in such nonsense! This is occultism cloaked with a veil of Biblical jargon.

---

[117] Acts 19:17-20 (emphasis added)

"Christian" Tarot Cards / Destiny Cards

This is another unbelievable practice found in some corners of Christianity. It is an utter disgrace that such practices find a home in some corners of the Christian faith.

One group insists that their "Destiny Cards" are not the same as Tarot cards. They go to New Age festivals with them in the name of evangelism. One article from ChristianPost.com explains the group this way,

> (They) describe themselves as "trained spiritual consultants," and say on their website that they "draw from the same divine energy of the Christ spirit."
>
> "We practice a form of supernatural healing that flows from the universal presence of the Christ. We draw from the same divine energy of the Christ spirit, as ancient followers did and operate only out of the third heaven realm to gain insight and revelation," they say.[118]

"Trained spiritual consultants," "universal presence," and "divine energy" are not Biblical terms. They are New Age terms. Once again, this is thinly veiled and coded occultism. It has no place in the life of the born-again child of God.

> *17 "Therefore, come out from their midst and be separate," says the Lord. "And do not touch what is unclean; And I will welcome you. 18 And I will be a father to you, And you shall be sons and daughters to Me," Says the Lord Almighty.[119]*

Dear saint, the Bible never endorses the use of worldly or other worldly practices as a means of evangelism.

---

[118] Christianpost.com/news (parenthesis added)
[119] 2 Corinthians 6:17-18

The Color Run

In recent years, many churches have begun offering their young people a "Christianized" or secular version of Hindu's Holi Festival.

The Holi Festival is paganism through and through. There are no two ways about it!

In short, it is Hindu's story of the triumph of good over evil. I will not give a detailed explanation of it here because doing so would require me to name some of the Hindu gods to whom this pagan festival pays homage; something I am unwilling to do. It is, nevertheless, undeniably, irreversibly, and inextricably pagan and cannot be "redeemed" simply by changing the name and parabolic meaning to something "Christian."

Christian churches call it by its Western name, "The Color Run." They have served it up to their teenagers, youth groups and young adults as just a fun activity. It looks like loads of innocent fun to young people as they run around and throw colored powder on each other. What could possibly be the harm in this fun event?

But churches are softening up the younger generation to embrace occultic and pagan practices, albeit naively enough perhaps. The subliminal influence is real and dangerous. In their desperate attempt to impress, they give these pagan practices new meanings by adding a verse or two from the holy Word of God as cover.

Lord, have mercy!

Self-Help, New Age, Wicca, Yoga, Yin-Yang, Zodiac, Horoscope, Meditation, Kung Fu, Karate, Judo, Hinduism, Buddhism, etc.

Except for Wicca, which is a form of witchcraft, all of these practices are inextricably rooted Eastern religions. They are occultic and there is no place for them in the life of a New Testament guided disciple of Jesus Christ. Still, so many Postmodern Christians today consider them harmless or even a help and boost to their spirituality. They do not understand that they are exposing themselves to the very dark playground of demonic activity.

Too many Christians today are willing to share, quote and post from New Age, Wicca, Buddhist, and other self-help sources. I grieve every time I see a Christian posting a "feel good" self-help quote, perhaps including a picture of someone sitting in the lotus position. I cringe even more when the one posting is a minister of the Gospel of Jesus Christ... sometimes, even Full Gospel ministers!

Why would the child of God turn to television and movie stars, Confucius, Buddha, Gandhi, etc. for inspirational quotes?

The Postmodern Church is so hungry to be fed and inspired by ungodly people and false belief systems, but God's Word and the anointed written and spoken preaching and teaching that flows from that Word contains all the help and inspiration we could ever need!

> *8 See to it, then, that no one enslaves you by means of the worthless deceit of human wisdom, which comes from the teachings handed down by human beings and from the ruling spirits of the universe, and not from Christ.*[120]

Pastors and Christian ministers must faithfully deliver the Word of God to their audiences... not occultism, Eastern religion, and the philosophies of *men* dressed up in Christian terms!

Universalism and Ultimate Reconciliation

This abominable lie has been around for a long time, but it fits so well into the Postmodern philosophical family.

To put it simply, this doctrine teaches that God will ultimately reconcile all *mankind* to Himself. It doesn't matter if a person accepted Christ in this life or not because everyone will ultimately be with God in heaven anyway, the idea being that God is sooooooo loving that He is incapable of allowing anyone to spend eternity in tormenting hell.

---

[120] Colossians 2:8 GNT Bible

I used to warn our Bible School students in the Philippines way back in the '80s to beware of this dangerous doctrine.

The story that Jesus told of the rich man and Lazarus in Luke 16:19-31 is proof enough for us of the existence of a real place of eternal torment called Hades or hell.

Every activity described in this chapter is an example of all that the believer must renounce and abandon once they have come to Christ.

All these practices and philosophies are not just unscriptural, they are actually anti-scriptural. Practicing them opens up one's life to the demonic supernatural paranormal realm which is forbidden in Scripture. All these are an abomination to God.

There is no place for these false doctrines and occultic activities in Biblical Christianity.

CHAPTER TEN

MORAL RELATIVISIM AND SITUATION ETHICS

Jesus said to him, "I am <u>the Way</u>, and <u>the Truth</u>, and <u>the Life; no one</u> comes to the Father, but through Me.
John 14:6 (emphasis added)

Have you ever heard the phrase, "grading on the curve?" If you are a teacher, you probably know what this phrase means. When teachers grade their students' work, they must first establish the standard by which all test papers or work will be graded. Sometimes, teachers use a system called, "grading on the curve." Here is how it works:

Let's say a civics teacher gives a 20 point "True or False" quiz to a class of 30 students. First, the teacher will grade each test paper individually based on the fixed answers of either True or False. But rather than have fixed, pre-determined grade brackets by which all grades are recognized, instead, the teacher throws out the papers with the best (highest) and worst (lowest) scores and then averages all the other scores together. Based upon the average of the scores of the entire class (minus the highest and lowest), the teacher develops a standard for what the "A,"

"B," "C" grade brackets will be for that quiz. The design of this system is to help "even out" everyone in the class. The student whose paper was thrown out because they had the lowest score, receives a lift in their grade. However, the student who had the highest score paper (a perfect test score, for example) now unfairly has a lower-than-perfect value of their work. The new "A" is now based on a points level somewhere lower than the perfect score of 100%. In percentages, maybe 96% or 94% is the new "100%." The student who earned a perfect score will still receive an "A," but it is no longer worth the 100% perfection he or she earned. There is no perfect score, no 100%, when grading on the curve. This is good news for everyone except the student who earned a perfect score and deserved a grade commensurate to that score.

In a Modern-Postmodern world literally everything and everyone is graded on the curve because there are no fixed absolutes for life, fairness, and morality. Moral anarchy breeds and flourishes in the atmosphere of Postmodernism.

God Doesn't Grade on the Curve

The devil has fed the world two dangerous and distinct lies.

The first is that everyone on earth is a "child of God." How often do we hear people making this claim when they say, "We are all children of God?"

It exposes their lack of knowledge in God's Word. Only when a person is born-again through acceptance and profession of faith in Jesus Christ, does that person become a part of God's family.[121]

The second lie is that every person is "basically good in their heart."

Randomly ask just about anyone walking down the street if they think of themselves as being a good person. Most of time, the answer will come back to you sounding something like this:

---

[121] John 3:3-7; Romans 10:9-13; 2 Corinthians 5:17, 13:5

"Yes, I think I am basically a good person. Okay, maybe not as good as Mother Theresa but certainly not as bad as a murderer or terrorist."

That is grading on the curve.

Unfortunately for every person counting on self-goodness as a means to an eternal paradise, the standard demanded by God for a right relationship with Him and entrance into His heavenly Kingdom is 100% flawless perfection. But the Bible teaches us that no one in all of human history, except Jesus Christ, earned a perfect 100% score in life.

Romans 3:10 says,

> *there is <u>none</u> righteous, <u>no not one</u>. (emphasis added)*

And in verse 23,

> *for <u>all</u> have sinned and fallen short of the glory of God. (emphasis added)*

Again, in Isaiah we read,

> *<u>all</u> our righteousness are as filthy rags (before God).[122] (emphasis added)*

The word "righteousness" means having a right relationship with God. It also refers to the intrinsic moral character and goodness of a person. Left to ourselves, none of us even come close to 100% righteous or perfect. No one meets God's demand for flawless perfection in holiness. That is why the devil has convinced *man* to institute the fake system of "grading on the curve" for the governance of moral behavior. Satan's fake moral grading system can be found in all three socio-philosophical eras. This curve-grading system adapts and expresses itself differently in each of the three eras. However, this philosophy really took hold in earnest with the transition into the Modern Era.

A good example in the Bible of how people try to grade their lives "on the curve" is the parable that Jesus told of the Pharisee and the Tax Collector in Luke 18:9-14:

---

[122] Isaiah 64:6 KJV (emphasis added)

9 And He also told this parable to some people who trusted in themselves that they were righteous, and viewed others with contempt: 10 "Two men went up into the temple to pray, one a Pharisee and the other a tax collector. 11 The Pharisee stood and was praying this to himself: 'God, I thank You that I am not like other people: swindlers, unjust, adulterers, or even like this tax collector. 12 I fast twice a week; I pay tithes of all that I get.' 13 But the tax collector, standing some distance away, was even unwilling to lift up his eyes to heaven, but was beating his breast, saying, 'God, be merciful to me, the sinner!' 14 I tell you, this man went to his house justified rather than the other; for everyone who exalts himself will be humbled, but he who humbles himself will be exalted."

The Pharisee presumed that he was more acceptable to God because of his self-righteous piousness. He graded himself and the Tax Collector "on the curve" and decided he was better than the Tax Collector. Tax Collectors were scum in the eyes of the people because they were often dishonest extortioners in the collection of taxes. But in this case, it was the humble Tax Collector, and not the religious Pharisee, who came away with forgiveness from God.

For the better part of 5,500 years, there was an instinctive, intrinsic "knowing" in every person that *man* is a sinner, imperfect and accountable to a greater, unseen Power. But liberal, politically correct Postmodern philosophy has baked into *man's* consciousness the lie that there are no fixed standards for right and wrong, good and evil, truth and error. I have watched this instinctive knowing fade from traditional American culture and life over the past 30 years. It is sad to watch.

In the mind of this Postmodern, politically correct, Millennial generation, you are simply labeled "old-fashioned," "out-of-touch," "ignorant," and "judgmental" at best if you believe in absolutes. At worst, you are labeled the enemy. You are falsely accused of being misogynist, homophobic, and every other name in the book, simply for the unforgiveable offense of believing in fixed, moral absolutes. The Postmodern world is a world of moral and ethical relativism. What a mess of gobbledygook!

Modernists and Postmodernists require acceptance and tolerance from everyone else but prove to be some of the most intolerant people in society! They are incapable of simply "agreeing to disagree" and letting the topic rest there. No, they demand subjection from the believer. The believer is expected to relent from his/her convictions and embrace the Modern-Postmodern position or there will be retribution to pay!

This is the spirit of untruth. This is the spirit of the father of lies.[123] This is the spirit of anti-christ.[124]

In Acts 7:54-60, we read the story of the death of Stephen. Stephen is the first recorded Christian martyr.

> *54 Now when they heard this, they were cut to the quick, and they <u>began gnashing their teeth</u> at him. 55 But being full of the Holy Spirit, he gazed intently into heaven and saw the glory of God, and Jesus standing at the right hand of God; 56 and he said, "Behold, I see the heavens opened up and the Son of Man standing at the right hand of God." 57 But they cried out with a loud voice, and <u>covered their ears</u> and rushed at him with one impulse. 58 When they had driven him out of the city, they began stoning him; and the witnesses laid aside their robes at the feet of a young man named Saul. 59 They went on stoning Stephen as he called on the Lord and said, "Lord Jesus, receive my spirit!" 60*

---

[123] John 8:44

[124] I John 2:22; 4:1-3; II John 1:7

Then falling on his knees, he cried out with a loud voice, "Lord, do not hold this sin against them!" Having said this, he fell asleep. (emphasis added)

The Scribes and Pharisees couldn't stand to listen to the truth that Stephen was preaching so they gnashed their teeth at him, covered their ears, rushed at him with one impulse and stoned him to death. This Premodern Age religious mob was acting just like the intolerance of the Postmodern influenced individual and mobs we see in our news every day... lashing out in furious anger at anyone who dares to disagree with their "reality."

Truly mature and tolerant people can agree to disagree without being disagreeable. When we attempt to share the Gospel with someone, we do not do so at the point of a knife or gun. Scripture mandates that we share the Gospel,[125] the Good News of salvation through the redemptive work of Jesus Christ,[126] to make disciples for Him,[127] and to give an account of the hope that lies within us.[128] However, nowhere does God's Word instruct us to force people to accept this wonderful, needful gift of salvation.[129] Nowhere does God tell us to fight, debate, maim, defame, torture, cancel, persecute, or kill those who reject us and our message!

When the love of Christ controls a heart, there is no room for hate and intolerance. In fact, the most severe recourse we are instructed to take by the Lord Jesus Christ when someone rejects our Gospel message is to merely "shake the dust off our feet" and move on to share the Gospel with the next person![130] In other words,

---

[125] Romans 1:14-17
[126] Romans 10:9-16
[127] Matthew 28:18-20
[128] I Peter 3:15
[129] Luke 10:16
[130] Matthew 10:14; Luke 10:16; John 15:18-25

> **Shaking the dust off one's feet conveys the same idea as our modern phrase 'I wash my hands of it.' Shaking the dust off the feet is a symbolic indication that one has done all that can be done in a situation and therefore carries no further responsibility for it.**[131]

Not kill, decapitate, torture, hold a gun to, publicly shame and "cancel," ruin their reputation, demand their firing, etc.

Generally speaking, the unsaved man or woman indoctrinated by Modernist and Postmodernist philosophy has no capacity to do this! You see, the word "tolerance" to the Modern- Postmodern and the child of God means very different things.

When a Christian or conservative person uses the term tolerance, it simply means "to recognize the other person's belief or lifestyle without sharing those views."

In other words, "You have the right to believe that or live that way, but I do not share those views with you."

> **For example, someone is a Christian and someone is a Muslim. You understand what they believe, but you don't share their particular view, so you live and let live.**
>
> **However, [the Postmodern definition of] tolerance… is recognizing everyone's beliefs are equal, and that no truth claim is greater than another. All beliefs are tolerated since none can actually be 'the truth.'** [132]

The Bible teaches us to live by the first definition of tolerance as described above, but Modern and Postmodern culture demands subjection to the second definition in the above quote.

---

[131] gotquestions.org/shake-dust-off-feet

[132] bradalles.com/tolerance-and-post-modernism (brackets added)

Moral Relativism

Moral Relativism is the view that ethical standards, morality, and positions of right or wrong are culturally based and therefore, subject to a person's individual choice. In other words, everyone decides for themselves what is right and wrong.

Moral Relativism says, "If what I am doing is good in my own eyes and I don't feel guilty about it or hurt anyone else by doing it, then what I am doing is not bad or a sin."

A common example is when two people engage in premarital sex, justifying that it's their own private lives, that it is accepted as normal in society today, and anyway, they will be getting married in a few days, or weeks, or months... or years.

Moral Relativism is just as wrong when used by the self-righteous as it is when used by the man or woman who is immoral, amoral, and devoid of conscience because of their rejection of Jesus Christ. Once again, the parable of the Pharisee and Tax Collector in Luke 18 is a good example in Scripture of how moral relativism works through self-righteous attitudes. The Modern and Postmodern world simply took moral relativism to new heights, forcing its acceptance as "mainstream."

A research poll conducted in 2016 by the Barna Research Group entitled, "U.S. Barna Survey: Goodbye Absolutes, Hello New Morality," sheds some light on the current views or temperature of morality in America:

> **However, when it comes to the agreeing on what determines right and wrong, Americans are far from standing in unison.**
>
> **According to a majority of American adults (57 percent), knowing what is right or wrong is a matter of personal experience, Barna researchers assert.**
>
> **This view is much more prevalent among younger generations than among older adults, [as] three-quarters of**

Millennials (74 percent) agree strongly or somewhat with the statement, 'Whatever is right for your life or works best for you is the only truth you can know,' compared to only 38 percent of Elders. And Millennials (31 percent) are three times more likely than Elders (10 percent) and twice as likely as Boomers (16 percent) and Gen X-ers (16 percent) to strongly agree with the statement.

Practicing Christians are much less likely to agree with the moral relativist statement.

"The proportions of practicing Christians who disagree (59 percent) and agree (41 percent) that the only truth one can know is whatever is right for one's own life are the inverse of the general population (44 percent disagree, 57 percent agree)," the study found. "The difference is even more pronounced when practicing Christians (41 percent) are compared with adults of no faith, two-thirds of whom agree (67 percent) that the only truth one can know is whatever is right for one's own life."

With multiculturalism being taught in schools, many Americans are led to believe that morals are determined by one's cultural upbringing.

About two-thirds of all-American adults (65 percent) agree either strongly or somewhat (18 percent and 47 percent respectively) that 'every culture must determine what is acceptable morality for its people,' those conducting the study informed. "Again, Millennials (25 percent) are more likely than Elders (16 percent), Boomers (14 percent) or Gen X-ers (16 percent) to strongly agree with this view."[133]

---

[133] onenewsnow.com

This study reveals the extent of the decay in the acceptance of absolute moral standards in American culture.

The website, moral-relativism.com, backs-up the foregoing data with this explanation of moral relativism:

> **Moral relativism has steadily been accepted as the primary moral philosophy of modern society, a culture that was previously governed by a "Judeo-Christian" view of morality. While these "Judeo-Christian" standards continue to be the foundation for civil law, most people hold to the concept that right or wrong are not absolutes but can be determined by each individual. Morals and ethics can be altered from one situation, person, or circumstance to the next. Essentially, moral relativism says that anything goes, because ultimately life is without meaning. Words like "ought" and "should" are rendered meaningless. In this way, moral relativism makes the claim that it is morally neutral.[134]**

Weeeee! It is easy to understand now why the phrase, "thou shalt not..." from God's Word is the biggest offender of all to the moral relativist!

Moral Relativism Leads to Moral Equivalence

Moral equivalence is the false belief that two sides of any issue always have precisely the same moral correctness or value. Neither of the two compared sides can ever claim to be greater or more moral than the other. Let me give you some examples:

1 is a number. 2 is a number. So 1 = 2. But, of course, every rational person knows that 1 and 2 are not of equal value even though they are both numbers. 2 is greater than 1, but not according to moral equivalence.

---

[134] moral-relativism.com

The terrorist organization, Hamas, initiates the firing of rockets at Israel in the hopes of killing innocent Israeli civilians. But, when Israel responds as they must in protecting their people, governments from around the world tell both sides to deescalate. The truth that world leaders fail to acknowledge is one side's rockets are fired without provocation to kill, while Israel's use of retaliatory firing is the defensive security of its citizenry. There is no moral equivalence between these two positions.

Or, how about in a local church when an Absalom-type person tears up a church and then leaves with slander on their lips against the pastor all the way out the door, and then other people tell the pastor that mediation is needed where both sides admit their (morally equivalent) "failures" in the relationship... They push that the conduct of the wolf in sheep's clothing (i.e.: rebellion, slander, etc.) is morally equivalent to the pastor's counteractions taken under his God-given authority and responsibility in protecting the remaining sheep within from that wolf. They are not morally equivalent.

Finally, let's talk marriage and divorce. Let's say that Spouse A had multiple affairs during their marriage to Spouse B who had only been faithful. Often times, Spouse A will insist that their marriage broke up because "both sides are equally to blame." Spouse A insists that the small potatoes shortcomings of Spouse B rise in moral equivalence to the very horrible sin of adultery... but of course, they are not at all of the same moral severity.

Moral Relativism Leads to Selective Moral Outrage

Another problem with moral relativism is that it also justifies violence or sin if the commission of such have as their reason or goal the defense of their strongly held views on a matter.

"The end justifies the means. If you are not in agreement with me on an issue (for example), then my rage and violence towards you are completely morally justified," is their reasoning.

Our lives are plum full of instances of this today. The news overflows daily with reports about groups of ideological thugs who riot, loot, burn, and destroy public and private businesses, buildings, and monuments declaring the terror and destruction their outrage causes are morally justified because they destroy for a greater "just cause." But there is no concern or outrage from the looters over the private property and businesses which have been destroyed. This is selective moral outrage.

Uncontested is the fact that humans across all three socio-philosophical eras have practiced these philosophical sins because of sin in the heart of *man*, but Postmodernism has given these heightened meaning, prominence, and expression in society today.

Situation Ethics

Joined at the hip so-to-speak to Moral Relativism is the equally problematic philosophy of Situation Ethics.

Basically, situation ethics can be defined as,

> **The doctrine of flexibility in the application of moral laws according to circumstances. A system of ethics by which acts are judged within their contexts instead of by categorical principles.**[135]

I first heard this term during the one year I spent in the Lutheran Liberal Arts college in Texas called Texas Lutheran College back in 1979-80. The professor of a class on Religious Education insisted that we accept and apply situation ethics as the standard for understanding human behavior. Then he gave this example:

Both parents of a young girl about 14 years old die, leaving her alone to care for 3 younger siblings. Without any relatives to help them, this girl enters into a life of prostitution in order to get money to care for her

---

[135] https://en.wikipedia.org/wiki/Situational_ethics

younger brothers and sisters. Situation ethics requires that the girl be hailed as a selfless hero because of how she sacrificed herself in that situation. Anyone who dares to call the decision and actions of this girl sinful is the real villain.

So, even as far back as 40 years, the philosophies of Moral Relativism and Situation Ethics were in full swing infiltrating *man's* consciousness and corrupting *his* worldview.

In short, Modernism and Postmodernism leave *man* with a corrupted sense of morality at best. At worst, these leave *him* completely devoid of any sort of moral compass altogether.

One might argue that humans have always thought this way, but not to the prevalent degree they are today. Go back to the year 1897 and you will find proof that Biblical standards of absolute right and wrong still held fast even in secular literature. I am referring to the famous novel, *Jane Eyre*, by Charlotte Bronte.

Jane Eyre was not written as a Christian story. It is simply one of the most famous secular novels ever written in British literature. In it, the main character, Jane Eyre, is orphaned at a young age and subsequently tossed from one home to another because no one really wanted to have to take care of her. Hers is a sort of Cinderella role in these homes where she is made to do hard work day and night to earn her keep. Somehow, she is able to secure an education as a teacher, so she takes a job as a live-in teacher. Her student is the spoiled young daughter of a very wealthy businessman who is rarely ever home. Long story short, eventually in the course of time, this businessman and Jane Eyre fall in love. He asks her to marry him, and she thinks that finally something good is happening to her life.

But while standing at the altar, the pastor asks the famous wedding question, "Is there anyone who objects to the marriage of this man to this woman?"

Suddenly, a man steps out from the shadows in the back of the chapel, speaks up and says in effect (not a quote from the book), "Should this man (referring to Jane's betrothed) marry a second time when he already has a wife who is insane and locked up in the attic of his mansion?"

Well, Jane knew nothing of all that, so she runs out of the church and locks herself in her bedroom.

It is here where we pick up the story as she wrestles with her own conscience. There is a part of her that wants to justify marrying this man anyway but the morally guided part of her won't have any of it! Here is how she wrestled within herself and came to her conclusion to flee the man and his mansion because there was in her a moral foundation which would not allow her to justify adultery and polygamy no matter how justifiable both seemed in that situation:

> **... 'Who in the world cares for you? Or who will be injured by what you do?'**
>
> **Still indomitable was the reply: 'I care for myself. The more solitary, the more friendless, the more unsustained I am, the more I will respect myself. I will keep the law given by God; sanctioned by man. I will hold to the principles received by me when I was sane, and not mad as I am now. Laws and principles are not for times when there is no temptation: They are for such moments as this, then body and soul rise in mutiny against their rigour; stringent they are; inviolate they shall be. If at my individual convenience I might break them, what would be their worth? They have a worth – so I have always believed; and if I cannot believe it now, it is because I am insane... Preconceived opinions, foregone determinations are all I have at this hour to stand by; there I plant my foot.[136]**

---

[136] Jane Eyre by Charlotte Bronte, published in 1897, page 344

I love this quote. I hope you can get past the old English writing style. Can you see that even in the secular novels of that Premodern era, authors and the characters they created accepted moral absolutes as a given. The moral matters of life were black or white, wrong or right. No gray area. No moral relativism. No situation ethics.

This is what is missing in the soul of *man* today thanks to Modern and Postmodern philosophy.

Jane Eyre flees and wanders for a few years. In the meantime, the mansion of the wealthy businessman catches fire. He loses literally everything in the fire including his lunatic wife who dies in the fire. Only he and his daughter survive although he becomes crippled from the fire.

After some years, the paths of the now poor and crippled businessman and Jane Eyre cross again. Their romance is rekindled, and they eventually get married. She could now marry the man she loved with a clear conscience. She had nothing to do with the fire, neither did she plot or desire harm towards the insane wife.

But the story is meant to show how Jane Eyre was, in a sense, vindicated and rewarded for her own moral scruples. What a story! But you won't find many secular novels in this cultural atmosphere with a great storyline like that!

Sadly, characters today are hailed as the heroes more for their immorality, moral relativism and situation ethics, than any scruples they may possess. In so many of Hollywood's movies today, the lawbreakers are portrayed as the good guys and those who should be cast as the "good guys" are cast instead as weak, inept, and corrupt.[137]

Our world has slipped from the gutter of liberal Modernism into the deeper gutter of progressive Postmodern philosophy so quickly.

Mankind believed in the absolute existence of God (or at least a supernatural "higher power") and in absolute truth for nearly 6,000

---

[137] Isaiah 5:20

years. But now, in a span of around just 500 years or less, we have moved from believing that God and truth exist... to God and truth do not exist... and then to the worst position of all: "no one knows anything for sure."

CHAPTER ELEVEN

DON'T HURT MY FEELINGS

> **"**
>
> *But we preach Christ crucified, to Jews a stumbling block,*
> *and to Gentiles foolishness, but to those who are the*
> *called, both Jews and Greeks, Christ is the power of God*
> *and the wisdom of God.*
> *1 Corinthians 1:23-24*

Generation Snowflake (Snowflake-ism)

Being a genuine disciple of Jesus Christ is not for the faint of heart. Hardship and suffering are part of the Gospel package. By hardship and suffering, we mean that because true disciples of Jesus Christ live under the authority of God's Word and not the standards of the world around us, we should expect to experience rejection and discrimination and sometimes worse because of our faith and values.

There are many verses in the New Testament which explain this to the believer. Consider these:

> *Indeed, all who desire to live godly in Christ Jesus will be*
> *persecuted. 2 Timothy 3:12*

For it is better, if God should will it so, that you suffer for doing what is right rather than for doing what is wrong. 1 Peter 3:17

If you are insulted for the name of Christ, you are blessed, because the Spirit of glory, and of God, rests upon you. 15 Make sure that none of you suffers as a murderer, or thief, or evildoer, or a troublesome meddler; 16 but if anyone suffers as a Christian, he is not to be ashamed, but is to glorify God in this name. 1 Peter 4:14-16

Blessed are those who have been persecuted for the sake of righteousness, for theirs is the kingdom of heaven. 11 "Blessed are you when people insult you and persecute you, and falsely say all kinds of evil against you because of Me. 12 Rejoice and be glad, for your reward in heaven is great; for in this same way they persecuted the prophets who were before you. Matthew 5:10-12

Biblical faith does not teach us to go around looking for trouble; that's the devil's way of doing things.[138] Rather, our faith in Christ strengthens us in the face of trouble, persecution and suffering.[139]

Generally speaking, Millennials and Gen Z-ers are notorious for being soft-skinned. They look for constant approving affirmation. They have grown up with a fairly easy life so many crumble under the slightest opposition or hardship. They are not accustomed to suffering. This makes them as fragile as a snowflake; able to hear only what agrees with them and makes them feel good.

---

[138] 1 Peter 5:8

[139] John 16:33; Ephesians 6:10-12; 2 Corinthians 12:9-10; 1 Peter 5:9-10

Postmodernism requires the immediate blocking of any words that disagree with, challenge, correct, or bring conviction to a person's conscience. Because Biblical truth does all of these, it is considered the worst "hate speech" of all in the mind of the Modernist and Postmodernist. Even when the Gospel presentation focuses on the love of God, the Postmodernist must cover their ears for the love of God ultimately calls us to repentance and life transformation.

In our world today, free speech is only acceptable if the opinion delivered affirms the "I'm okay, you're okay" narrative. Any speech which challenges or contradicts Postmodern positions is silenced as "hate speech." There is no room for competing ideas. No debate and no tolerance for opposing views.

Consider the following Postmodern sentiments which are accepted as "the norm" in our world today:

"You have to accept me as I am."

"I am me and will never surrender that."

"I will never be wrong in being who I am."

Allow me to translate these Postmodern phrases for you. What they really say is, "Don't you dare tell me I'm wrong."

In the Postmodern dictionary, the word "accept" means that the hearer must completely embrace and endorse the speaker's behavior, conduct, lifestyle, or opinion. The Postmodernist must have total affirmation. Simply agreeing to disagree and then leaving the other person to their choices while holding an opposing viewpoint is unacceptable.

Here is a very disturbing example of the Postmodern demand for total subjection to sinful lifestyle choices.

The Canadian government jailed a father for the "sin" of voicing his disapproval over his minor age biological daughter's decision to transition to a boy and his disagreement with the local authorities' support of her decision to transition without notifying or gaining the approval of the parents ahead of time.

In their decision, the justices of the B.C. Court of Appeals ruled the father could not voice his opposition to his daughter's decision and was warned any attempt to pressure his child to change course would be considered a form of family violence, punishable by law. Chief Justice Robert Bauman and Justice Barbara Fisher said the dad's "refusal to accept" his teenage daughter's choices "is troublesome," adding that his failure to fully endorse his kid's desire for irreversible transgender treatments has caused the minor "significant pain" that has "resulted in a rupture of what both parties refer to as an otherwise loving parent-child relationship."

"The "rupture," the justices added, is not in the child's "best interests."

"With that in mind, Bauman and Fisher ordered the father to refer to his biological daughter only by male pronouns and barred him from speaking to members of the media."[140]

The father is ordered, by law, to not only passively accept his daughter's transition but rather to actually approve of it and celebrate it. His own dissenting opinion is silenced and outlawed.

When wrong can't win an argument, its only recourse is to silence the opposing voice.

I can only imagine the anguish this father must be experiencing. So many legal and God-given moral rights stripped from him by a Postmodern-laced judicial system.

Lord, have mercy on all parents today!

---

[140] Canadian Father Jailed for Speaking Out Against Biological Daughter's Gender Transition – Faithwire.com

In the Postmodern world, absolutes are the enemy. Swimming against the current of Modern-Postmodern culture is Postmodernism's unpardonable, intolerable sin.

As has already been noted, God does indeed "accept" us as we are when we come to Him. There is no prerequisite of "self-help clean-up" first. Jesus made His invitation absolutely clear in Matthew 11:28-30,

> *28 Come to Me, all who are weary and heavy-laden, and I will give you rest. 29 Take My yoke upon you and learn from Me, for I am gentle and humble in heart, and you will find rest for your souls. 30 For My yoke is easy and My burden is light.*

"Come just as you are," is the invitation of the Savior. And then the Bible shines the spotlight on just exactly "how we are" when we do come to Him with these immortal words,

> *23 For all have sinned and fallen short of the glory of God.*[141]

And,

> *8 while we were yet sinners, Christ died for us.*[142]

This is the true and absolute condition of every man, women and child before Christ and without Him regardless the socio-philosophical epoch.

But here is the absolute Good News in 2 Corinthians 5:17,

> *17 Therefore, if any man be in Christ, he is a new creation; the <u>old is passed away</u> and behold, all things <u>have become new</u>. (emphasis added)*

He loves and accepts (i.e.: receives) us as we are when we come to Him but, praise God, He loves us enough not to leave us in the same condition that we came to Him!

---

[141] Romans 3:23
[142] Romans 5:8

The promises God made to Israel in Ezekiel 36 are also for you and me:

> *25 Then I will sprinkle clean water on you, and you will be clean; I will cleanse you from all your filthiness and from all your idols. 26 Moreover, I will give you a new heart and put a new spirit within you; and I will remove the heart of stone from your flesh and give you a heart of flesh. 27 I will put My Spirit within you and cause you to walk in My statutes, and you will be careful to observe My ordinances. 29 Moreover, I will save you from all your uncleanness; and I will call for the grain and multiply it, and I will not bring a famine on you. 31 Then you will remember your evil ways and your deeds that were not good, and you will loathe yourselves in your own sight for your iniquities and your abominations. (emphasis added)*

Sincere remorse over and abandonment of our former manner of life is generated by the new heart and spirit we receive in the new birth as we confess Jesus Christ as Lord.

From the Old Testament to the New, redemption involves life transformation![143]

We are not supposed to brag about "being who we are." Instead, wisdom speaks to our hearts to humble ourselves under the mighty hand of God and to invite the Holy Spirit to work in our life, helping us to shed what is displeasing in God's sight and embrace all that is new in Christ.[144]

The Bible tells the believer in Christ to put something "off" and put something better from God "on" in its place,

---

[143] 2 Corinthians 3:16-18
[144] Ephesians 5:10; 2 Corinthians 5:9

22 that, regarding your previous way of life, you put off your
old self [completely discard your former nature], which is
being corrupted through deceitful desires,
24 and put on the new self [the regenerated and renewed
nature], created in God's image... in the righteousness and
holiness of the truth [living in a way that expresses to God
your gratitude for your salvation].[145]

Cooperating with the Holy Spirit brings about transformation in us from glory to glory.[146] This begins at the new birth and continues on for the rest of our lives on earth. This is the life of a true follower of Jesus Christ.

"You have no right to judge me." (Or "We have no right to judge them.")

Translation: "To tell me that I'm wrong or to disagree with me means you are judging me."

In the middle of Jesus' Sermon on the Mount, we find a very famous portion of Scripture. It has been misquoted and taken out of context by many who lack a comprehensive understanding of what Jesus is really saying:

1 Do not judge, so that you will not be judged. 2 For in the
way you judge, you will be judged; and by your standard of
measure, it will be measured to you. 3 Why do you look at the
speck that is in your brother's eye, but do not notice the log
that is in your own eye? 4 Or how can you say to your brother,
'Let me take the speck out of your eye,' and look, the log is in
your own eye? 5 You hypocrite, first take the log out of your

---

[145] Ephesians 4:22,24 AMP (emphasis added)
[146] 2 Corinthians 3:18

own eye, and then you will see clearly to take the speck out of your brother's eye![147]

These verses are championed by Postmodern Christians looking for Scriptural cover for their, "If it feels good, do it," and "I'm okay, you're okay," lifestyles.

A guilty conscience is no problem when these verses are taken out of context and employed to shield one's conscience from accountability.

Used in context, though, these verses are talking only about judging others through the lens of self-righteous hypocrisy.

For example, if a Christian is living in hidden sin, sleeping with someone they are not married to... and then they begin to criticize another believer, or unbeliever, about their immoral lifestyle, that is the kind of self-righteous, hypocritical judgmental behavior Jesus says is so wrong. The first person should deal with the "log" in their own life (i.e.: their own immorality) before trying to call out the other person for their sin (i.e.: the speck).

Christian author, Eric J. Bargerhuff, explains it this way in an excerpt from his book posted on Crosswalk.com:

> **Those who mishandle this verse often use it as a "shield for sin," a barrier to keep others at bay, allowing them to justify living as they please without any regard for moral boundaries or accountability. Their objections sound like this: "Aren't we all sinners? What gives us the right to make moral judgments about someone else? Isn't that God's job?"**
>
> **However, when we take a closer look at the context of Matthew 7 and the teachings of the rest of Scripture, it is clear that this verse cannot be used to substantiate unrestrained moral freedom, autonomy,**

---

[147] Matthew 7:1-5

and independence. This was not Jesus' intent. He was not advocating a hands-off approach to moral accountability, refusing to allow anyone to make moral judgments in any sense.

Quite the opposite, Jesus was explicitly rebuking the hypocrisy of the Pharisees, who were quick to see the sins of others but were blind and unwilling to hold themselves accountable to the same standard they were imposing on everyone else.[148]

In other words, there is clear context to these verses which must not be ignored and overlooked.

The Book of Proverbs is full of wisdom. Oft times, what people call "judging" is simply the work of standalone truth spotlighting a certain character or behavior as wrong. In that instance, it is not one person who is "judging" the other person but rather it is the Word of God identifying the sinful behavior and calling it out.

A parent came to me with her teenage daughter years ago for pastoral counselling. The parent was having trouble with the daughter's rebellious attitude. During our conversation together, I read several verses to her from Proverbs that perfectly described her rebellious behavior towards her parents.

The girl shot back as fast as she could with the Postmodern line, "You have no right to judge me."

I answered that I was not judging her at all but that the Word of God was calling out her conduct.

Then, I asked her the following question, "If you are standing under an apple tree and an apple falls next to you, would you be judging that piece of fruit if you call it an apple?"

---

[148] crosswalk.com/faith/bible-study/the-most-misused-verses-in-the-bibleexcerpt

"No," was her reply.

"Why?" I questioned again.

"Because it is obviously an apple and it fell from an apple tree," she again replied.

"In the same way that a person can identify an apple as an apple, the Bible also identifies the condition of our hearts and lives. It is not that we 'judge' the piece of fruit but merely identify it for what it clearly is. That is what the Word of God does for us. It identifies or locates our heart on any given issue and calls us out! It is the wise person who responds accordingly," was my explanation to her.[149]

She had no reply to that but sadly choose to continue in her rebellious ways.

"Mine is as good as yours."

"Mine" meaning, my belief, my religion (or lack thereof), my morals, my lifestyle, my conduct, my behavior, etc.

Translation: "You have no right to suggest that your belief, religion, morals, lifestyle, conduct, behavior, etc., is right or the truth but that mine is wrong. All beliefs and personal realities are equal, and all lifestyle decisions are equally moral."

But, of course, we have learned by this time, that is not true.

Each of the statement examples in this chapter are designed to block and preempt any and every potential incoming rebuke or correction.

It's not just that Postmoderns don't **want** to hear another point of view... it is that they **cannot bear** to hear anything less than total affirmation of whatever they have made to be as their own reality. When you hear someone say things like these statements, they are identifying themselves as having been influenced by or indoctrinated with Millennial, politically correct, Postmodern philosophy.

---

[149] Proverbs 9:9, 15:32

CHAPTER TWELVE

GOD'S STANDARD
OF MEASURE

> *For we are not bold to class or compare*
> *ourselves with some of those who commend themselves;*
> *but when they measure themselves*
> *by themselves, and compare themselves with themselves,*
> *they are without understanding.*
> *2 Corinthians 10:12*

So far, we have looked in great detail at how the Postmodernist formulates contrived (non)standards that enable them to justify their belief and lifestyles.

But what does the Bible say about how moral conduct is to be measured or decided? Just what is God's standard of measure?

Among the definitions for the word "judgment" is the meaning "a decision for or against something."

"To judge" means,

To form an opinion about something or someone after careful thought.[150]

---

[150] 1978 American Heritage Dictionary

The 1828 Webster Dictionary defines the word, *judge*, this way,

To compare facts or ideas, and perceive their agreement or disagreement, and thus to distinguish truth from falsehood.

So, all judgments begin as comparisons. A comparison means that you make a decision about one thing, person, or idea in connection with another.

We make comparisons all day long every day of our lives. We compare food, people, places, politics, situations, ideas, material things, etc. Those thumbs-up, thumbs-down decisions we make throughout each day as to the favorability or unfavourability of any given situation or topic then become the anchor for all our comparisons on that topic. Every comparison ends as a judgment.

Let's say, for example, that Tommy loves the color blue. He has made a ***decision*** about the color blue. In his estimation, no other color matches the greatness of blue because Tommy is ***comparing*** every other color with his favorite. All other colors come up short when ***compared*** to blue. Tommy has ***judged*** blue to be the best color. Blue is the ***standard*** by which he ***judges*** all other colors. Notice the words in bold-italic: decision, comparing, judged, standard… All these words interact like a chain reaction or domino effect.

If we make a very strong decision that we can't stand brussel sprouts, subconsciously we begin to judge all other vegetables by the anchor standard we have set which is our dislike of brussel sprouts. We will say,

"I like green beans but not brussel sprouts." Or,

"Corn is not too bad but brussel sprouts are horrible!"

Or when it comes to automobiles we might say something like, "Brand R is the best kind of car, but I would never buy a Brand H. They are awful!"

Personally, I am an Android and personal computer (PC) girl. I just don't get along with the Apple operating system. If I would use my own preference as the standard of measure in advising others when it comes to the Android/PC -vs- Apple/Mac debate, I would shout from the mountain top, "Android and PCs are unquestionably superior to Macs and iPhones!"

But, of course, that would not be true. The standard of measure I am using to make that judgment are my own experiences and preferences, not something objective, fixed, and inviolable.

Making decisions, comparisons, and judgments over the superficial matters of our everyday lives is quite normal and mostly harmless, "I like this, but not that."

The Wrong Standard of Measure

We get into trouble, though, when we take that same process and apply it to moral and legal matters; matters of faith, science and mathematics where absolutes are essential. Such important disciplines of life require fixed standards, not variable ones based on the ever changing whims of our own likes and dislikes, for in using variable standards we will inevitably end up establishing false standards by which we judge everything else in those areas. That is the point made in the verse at the beginning of this chapter.

Let's look again at Second Corinthians 10:12 through the lens of these translations:

12 Of course we would not dare classify ourselves or compare ourselves with those who rate themselves so highly. How stupid they are! They make up their own standards to measure themselves by, and they judge themselves by their own standards! GNT (emphasis added)

12 Oh, don't worry; we wouldn't dare say that we are as wonderful as these other men who tell you how important *they are! But they are only <u>comparing</u> themselves with each other, <u>using themselves as the standard of measurement</u>. How ignorant! NLT (emphasis added)*

12 Of course, we wouldn't dare to put ourselves in the same class or <u>compare</u> ourselves with those who rate themselves so highly. They <u>compare</u> themselves to one another and <u>make up their own standards to measure themselves by</u>, and then they <u>judge themselves by their own standards</u>. What self-delusion! TPT (emphasis added)

Paul was pushed to defend his apostolic ministry to the Corinthian believers. You see, the Corinthian church had gone gaga over false teachers who opposed Paul and his ministry. In the verse above, Paul explains that these false teachers were trying to prove their superiority over him. The problem was, they were commending themselves as having ministries superior to Paul's, but only because they compared themselves and their ministries to themselves. As a result, they judged themselves great, rather than to hold themselves and their ministries up to the fixed standard of the Word and Will of God. Paul calls this method of measurement "stupid, ignorant, and self-delusional." Ouch!

This explains perfectly how Postmodern belief and morality are decided. This is how moral relativism and situation ethics work.

In order for our "judgments" (opinions, decisions, and conclusions) to be accurate, first, our comparison must be accurate. And our "comparison" will only be accurate when it is based on a fixed and absolute anchor or standard of measure. It is a simple principle in mathematics and science:

If you begin with a wrong formula, you will end up with the wrong equation! If you begin with a false equation, you will end up with a false conclusion!

If we set ourselves and our own opinions as the anchor standard of measure by which we judge ourselves and everyone else, we will always judge ourselves, our motives and conduct, our ideas, our beliefs, our likes, etc., as approved. It has been well said that too often we judge others by their words and actions but ourselves by our intentions.

When we compare ourselves to others, we may feel proud because we think we are better. Conversely, we may be left feeling condemned and a failure because we don't have as much or haven't accomplished as much as the other person has.

Back in the 1980s, as my parents and I began to develop the Bible School ministry that God called us to build in the Philippines, we would often entertain American guests. They came over to help us. They would preach and teach. For the most part, this was a great blessing to us. But many would also share their opinions of our Bible School, and their unsolicited advice.

What made Mom, Dad, and me smile after multiple back-to-back sets of visitors were well on their way back home was the huge swing in the difference of opinions they formed about the ministry God led us to establish. Some visitors would gush over how great and how "big" our budding ministry was. Conversely, we could tell that others were just not impressed at all. They were polite but counting the minutes until they could go back home because our work was not shiny enough for them!

The feedback we received over many years of time ranged from, "Wow! Your ministry is so big, so impressive." To a yawn and passing comment, "Nice work, John. By the way, do you know Missionary So-and-So in Manila? They have a really huge work. They are famous back in the States… I want to get in touch with them. Can you help me?"

Mom, Dad, and I got used to it. In the opinion of some guests, we had the most outstanding mission work going in the whole world (not true, of course). And then to other guests, we were nothing more than a ho-hum and stepping stone to meet the star missionaries in the country!

But Mom, Dad, and I did not buy into either their praise or their shrug. We did not compare the ministry God had entrusted into our hands with that of another! We sought only for God's approval of what we were doing.

Two negative things happen every time we use ourselves as the standard of measure:

First, we will absolve ourselves of all guilt over sin and not properly repent from it. 1 John 1:8 warns against that,

> *If we say that we have no sin, we are deceiving ourselves, and the truth is not in us.*

Secondly, we will get stuck in the mud of one of two deep ditches. Either we will judge ourselves so small, insignificant and unworthy as a believer that the devil will walk all over us!

Or, we will end up with a head as big as a watermelon, swollen with pride. Either way, we will be in no condition to help anyone else!

The Word of God is the Only Standard of Measure

The Word of God, the Bible, is the only true and reliable, fixed and inviolable standard for our lives. When a thorough and objective consideration is given to it, the searcher will find that it alone qualifies, by every metric, to be the only credible standard of measure for life, belief, morality and conduct.

The Word of God says of itself in 2 Timothy 3:16,

> *16 All Scripture is <u>inspired by God</u> and profitable for teaching, for reproof, for correction, for training in righteousness. (emphasis added)*

The Amplified Translation puts it this way,

> *16 All Scripture is <u>God-breathed</u> [given by divine inspiration] and is profitable for instruction, for conviction [of sin], for correction [of error and restoration*

to obedience], for training in righteousness [learning to live in conformity to God's will, both publicly and privately— behaving honorably with personal integrity and moral courage]. (emphasis added)

When the Apostle Paul wrote this, he was referring to the 39 books of Old Testament scripture, but as the New Testament came into formation, that verse came to include the 27 books of the New Testament as well.

Hebrews 4:12 in the Amplified Translation says,

12 For the word of God is alive and full of power [making it active, operative, energizing, and effective]; it is sharper than any two-edged sword, penetrating to the dividing line of the breath of life (soul) and [the immortal] spirit, and of joints and marrow [of the deepest parts of our nature], exposing and sifting and analyzing and judging the very thoughts and purposes of the heart.

The Bible is a Book of books. It is not to be compared with any other book of religious belief. It stands alone in its uniqueness, character, and content.

The Old Testament was in place hundreds of years before Christ. The canon of New Testament scripture was finalized at the Council of Carthage in 397AD.

When we speak of the Canon of Scripture, we are referring to that collection of writings which constitute the authoritative and final norm or standard of faith and practice. This means that we think of the Word of God as the *measuring stick for our beliefs and our lives.* We use it to check our doctrine and our daily lifestyle.

The ancient Greek architects had an instrument that they used to measure various distances as they were designing and constructing a building. The instrument was a "canon;" a straight rod with marks set into its side, much like our modern rulers. It had to be unbendable and dependable as to its straightness.

The Greek word is κανόνας *kanónas* meaning "a cane, reed or rod." Strong's Exhaustive Dictionary of Old and New Testament Words says this about the word canon:

> κανών *kanōn;* from κάννα *kanna* (a straight rod); a rule, standard.

Anything that lined up with the standard of measure was considered "canon" or "established rule."[151]

Vine's Complete Expository Dictionary of Old and New Testament Words explains,

> kanon (κανών, 2583) originally denoted "a straight rod," used as a ruler or measuring instrument, or, in rare instances, "the beam of a balance," the secondary notion being either (a) of keeping anything straight, as of a rod used in weaving, or (b) of testing straightness, as a carpenter's rule; hence its metaphorical use to express what serves "to measure or determine" anything. By a common transition in the meaning of words, "that which measures," was used for "what was measured"; thus a certain space at Olympia was called a kanon...
>
> In general the word thus came to serve for anything regulating the actions of men, as a standard or principle. In Galatians 6:16, those who "walk by this rule (kanon)" are those who make what is stated in vv. 14 and 15 their guiding line in the matter of salvation through faith in Christ alone, apart from works, whether following the principle themselves or teaching it to others.

---

[151] Galatians 6:16

From this word came the idea of a body of truth or a rule of faith. Since Biblical Scripture contains, in written form, the true standard of faith, it came to be spoken of as "Canon," the rule against which *all* other books and writings must be judged.

Technically speaking, godly men did not *decide* on which writings were of divine origin and inspiration. Instead, they merely *recognized* them by putting them to the stringent test of canonical standards. These men dared not to rely upon their own opinions in doing their work.

Here is the important point to remember:

Canonization does not *make* a book into the Word of God. Rather, it is the process by which a writing is *recognized* as being of divine origin and inspiration and thus is included in the Word of God, the Bible.

Development of New Testament Canon

The standard used by the theologians at the Council of Carthage in 397AD as dozens upon dozens of writings from the first century were put to the canonical test included:

• Usage of the book or writing under consideration.

How well was the first century writer respected by the Body of Christ? Was the writing (book) significantly relied upon and passed around the Church world?

• Writer's relationship to Jesus and the Apostles.

The early Christians essentially asked, "Is this particular work under question the work of one of the apostles?" Or, "If it is not the work of the apostle himself, was it produced under the supervision of and with the stamp of approval of one of the apostles?"[152]

---

[152] lifeway.com/en/articles/bible-study-establishing-new-testament-canon

The godly men at the Council of Carthage took their assignment very seriously. Did the message of the writing being tested conform to the teaching of the original first century apostles? This was an essential requirement in the canonical process. You see, these church fathers wanted to make sure that the original teaching of apostles held fast and that no place was given for evolving theologies, teachings, and doctrines that deviated from the original apostolic writings and teachings.[153]

• Intrinsic Value and Message Quality.

Intrinsic means, "belonging to the real nature of a thing; not dependent on external circumstances; essential; inherent."

So any writing in the running to be included in New Testament Canon had to have high moral quality (the message must not condone sin), historical and geographical accuracy, and depth of message (simple enough for the seeker and new Christian to understand yet deep enough to keep the most dedicated scholar searching for more).

Further Proofs of Divine Origin and Inspiration

• Incalculable and Improbable Unity.

The entirety of God's Holy Word, the Bible, was written by some forty men over a period of 1,800 years; yet its message is completely unified. It has one central theme from Genesis to Revelation:

The redemptive plan of God for *mankind.*

Just try searching the internet for a list of books considered holy by their religions and you will find that all except the Bible were written by a single author. God did not entrust His self-revelation and the communication of His message to just one flawed man writing in one moment of time.

Sometimes opponents of Christianity say things like, "The Bible was written by men."

---

[153] Deuteronomy 4:2; Deuteronomy 12:32; Revelation 22:18; 1 John 4:1-6

That line is usually spouted by people who don't really know anything about the formation of Biblical Canon. It is uttered in ignorance. Their anti-Bible bias shows through in that they would never use the fact that the Quran, for example, which was truly written by just one man as a criticism of that book.

The men who were used by God to write were from all walks of life, including: prophets, priests and kings, judges, scribes, farmers, shepherds, poets and musicians, fishermen, a cupbearer, a tax collector, and a doctor.[154]

Their collective writing life span covered 1,800 years and only a few of them were contemporaries or knew one another. Yet, for all the diversity[155] in the list of writers, there is not even one contradiction in the complete message of God's Word.

Although the feelings of the writers may shine through at times, any perceived contradiction is simply due to a lack of understanding and revelation on the part of the reader.[156] The Word itself is infallible.

It is a mathematical impossibility that more than 40 men from all walks of life, most of whom did not know each other, could write a unified message over a period of 1,800 years. The odds of that happening by chance or human design are incalculable.

Only God's hand of direct involvement could orchestrate such a miracle as the Bible.

• Influence in the Affairs of Man.

The Bible has both influenced and altered the course of people's lives, nations, and even history itself as no other book has done. The Word of God never grows old or outdated. It's message is as fresh and relevant today as ever!

---

[154] 2 Peter 1:16,19-21; 1 John 1:1-4

[155] A beloved term among Postmoderns.

[156] 1 Corinthians 2:14

• Durability.

Psalm 119:89 says the Word of God is forever settled (fixed and established) in heaven.

In Matthew 24:35, Jesus said,

> *35 Heaven and earth will pass away, but My words will not pass away."*

For a thousand years, the Catholic Church tried to keep the Bible out of the reading reach of the masses in Europe; but the seeds of Reformation which took root in the fourteenth century blossomed into full Reformation by the 16th century *precisely because* of the durability of God's Word.

The invention of the Gutenberg Printing Press contributed greatly to the success of the Reformation of the Church. The Bible was the first book printed on Gutenberg's printing press in Mainz, Germany in 1455 and, for all practical purposes, was the first book ever printed in the world.

A quick internet search reveals that the entire Bible has been translated into at least 704 languages at the time of this writing and the New Testament in well over 1,500 additional languages.

The Bible topped the New York Times best seller list for so many years running since at least 1907 and deep into the 20th century that it is believed the NYT finally decided to discontinue mentioning it on their best sellers' lists.

The Bible Society estimates around 2.5 billion copies of the Bible were printed and distributed just between 1815-1975. And, they estimate that more than five billion Bibles have been printed and distributed in subsequent years.[157]

The Bible is far and away the most widely translated, printed, distributed and read book in the history of the world, bar none!

All this makes the Bible the number one literary target in the world for every unimaginable attack from the pit of hell, the goal being its

---

[157] guinnessworldrecords.com/world-records/best-selling-book-of-non-fiction

extermination, but all have failed... because of the Bible's divinely supernatural durability.

From Madalyn Murray O'Hair in America in the 1960s, to Islam, Fascism, Communism, Atheism, Witchcraft, Humanism, Modernism, Postmodernism, and every other "ism" inspired by hell and embraced by *man;* all have tried but will never defeat God's Holy Word.

While the whole world grapples with life under Postmodernism, Satan is using this evil philosophy to turn America into a Post-Christian country. With ferocious effort, enemies of the cross are battling harder than ever to rid America and the rest of world of the Word of God and Christian faith. Try as hard as the devil may, though, the Word of God is here to stay!

• Fulfilled Prophecy.

The Bible is the only book on earth that can tell what will happen before it happens and that with 100% accuracy.

It is estimated that between 25-33 Old Testament Messianic prophecies were fulfilled by our Lord Jesus Christ in just one hour of time on the day of His crucifixion.

H. Ross writes concerning Biblical fulfilled prophecy,

> **Unique among all books ever written, the Bible accurately foretells specific events -in detail- many years, sometimes centuries, before they occur. Approximately 2,500 prophecies appear in the pages of the Bible, about 2,000 of which already have been fulfilled to the letter— no errors.**
>
> **(The remaining 500 or so reach into the future and may be seen unfolding as days go by.) Since the probability for any one of these prophecies having been fulfilled by chance averages less than one in ten (figured very conservatively) and since the prophecies are for the most part independent of one another, the odds for all these prophecies having**

been fulfilled by chance without error is less than one in 10^{2000} (that is 10 with 2,000 zeros written after it)![158]

Incorruptible and Imperishable Words of Eternal Life

Luke 8:11 calls the Word of God a *"seed."* 1 Peter 1:23 says the seed is incorruptible and imperishable.

As we have already seen the word of God is described in Hebrews 4:12 as,

> *12 alive and full of power and sharper than any two-edged sword.*

The Bible is the most powerful book you will ever read.

When Jesus told the twelve disciples that they were free to stop following Him if they wanted to, Peter replied in a heartbeat,

> *68 Lord, to whom shall we go? You have the words of eternal life. 69 And we have already believed and have come to know that You are the Holy One of God.[159]*

Sincere investigation always opens one's heart to the authenticity and spiritual treasure trove of this divinely inspired book.

In the end, the only authority that counts is what God's Word says regarding the standard for governing right -vs- wrong, truth -vs- error, godliness -vs- evil, etc. No other book on the face of the earth can compare with God's Holy Word, the Bible. It is a supernatural book of divinely supernatural origin. No other book even comes close.

---

[158] reasons.org/explore/publications/tnrtb/read/tnrtb/2003/08/22/fulfilled-prophecy-evidence-for-the-reliability-of-the-bible

[159] John 6:67-69 (emphasis added)

The Perfect Law of Liberty

Each one of us must look into the mirror of God's Word, examine the condition of our own heart and be honest about what the Word mirror reflects back to us.[160] Examine your heart with these questions:

"How does my life measure up to what God's Word says? How am I measuring up to God's Will for my life? And, how does my character compare to the example set for me by Jesus Christ?"

To answer these questions correctly, it is necessary to be committed to the inerrancy of Scripture. To answer them honestly, we must be prepared to use the Word of God, and not ourselves, as the mirror into which we look and judge.

James 1 says,

> *21 Therefore putting aside all filthiness and all that remains of wickedness, in humility receive the word implanted, which is able to save your souls. 22 But prove yourselves doers of the word, and not merely hearers who delude themselves. 23 For if anyone is a hearer of the word and not a doer, he is like a man who looks at his natural face in a mirror; 24 for once he has looked at himself and gone away, he has immediately forgotten what kind of person he was. 25 But one who looks intently at the perfect law, the law of liberty, and abides by it, not having become a forgetful hearer but an effectual doer, this man shall be blessed in what he does.*

These verses in James teach us that God's Word is the only mirror that has the ability to accurately show us what the real state of our character and relationship is with God. Anything else we try to use, including ourselves, as the mirror for measuring our character, conduct, morality, heart, worth and intentions will be an imperfect mirror.

---

[160] 1 Corinthians 11:31; 2 Corinthians 13:5-8; Psalm 15:1-5

God's Word is the "the perfect law of liberty." Not liberty *to* sin or liberty from guilt, consequence and accountability when we do sin, but rather liberty to *not* sin! And freedom from trying to please God through religious observance of the Old Testament Law of Moses.[161] Although it is abundantly clear why one of the first goals worked on by Modernism was the elimination of the Ten Commandments from civil society. Why? Because they set forth a fixed and absolute standard for moral behavior. Because they are a mirror! That made the Ten Commandments one of Modern-Postmodern's top enemies.-

But these verses also teach us something else of equal importance. James, by the Holy Spirit, says here that if we are not living by the Word of God, then by default we are using ourselves as the mirror and standard of measure in judging our lives and others. Basically, he is saying that the only way we will be courageous enough to measure our lives by the fixed and inviolable Word of God is *if* we are practicing that very Word in our lives. Living by it, in other words.

Blessings await the person who is committed to living by the Word of God as his or her standard of measure:

1.   We will be blessed in whatever we do.[162]
2.   We will begin to see people the way God sees them.[163]
3.   We will be in a position to help others.[164]
4.   We will be promoted by God.[165]

What standard of measure are you using on yourself and others?

The only standard capable of an accurate measurement for faith, morality, character, and conduct is the mirror of God's Word. If you are living according to it, then all the rest for or against you in life is nothing more than fog and empty noise.

---

[161] Galatians 2:16; 3:2; 3:5; 3:21
[162] James 1:25
[163] 2 Corinthians 5:16
[164] Matthew 7:1-5; Galatians 6:1-5
[165] James 4:6-10; 1 Peter 5:5-6

Chapter Thirteen

WHEN TRUTH IS TRUE

> *Sanctify them in the truth; Thy word is truth.*
> John 17:17

The Modernist says, "Truth does not exist."

The Postmodernist says, "Who's to say whether or not truth exists? Nobody knows for sure."

But what does truth say about itself?

Whether the Modernist and Postmodernist like it or not, the truth is that truth exists!

Here are the characteristics of truth:

Truth is reality. It is always objective, never subjective. It is fixed, absolute, inviolable, immutable, and eternal. *All truth is.* Anything and everything that is true/truth is fixed, absolute, inviolable, unchangeable, and eternal. *Truth stands alone.* Untruth cannot. Truth needs no defense because it is simply "true."

Whether a person believes or denies the truth is irrelevant because whatever is true will always be true.

All truth is also fact, although not everything that is fact or factual is also automatically and equally truth. Truth is greater than and superior to facts. Facts are realities of the moment, but those realities are subject to change. Truth never changes! The Bible tells us that the physical realm is temporary (or "subject to change") but that the unseen realm is eternal.[166] Facts belong to the temporal realm. Truth belongs to the unseen, eternal realm. Everything in the natural realm is real, to be sure, but it is also subject to change. Truth, however, can never, will never change.

For example, the fact of the moment might be that you have suffered a betrayal, rejection or injustice from a husband, wife or other loved one and, as a result, you feel unloved and hopeless. Or perhaps a loved one or dear friend died, and you feel as if the whole world has collapsed around you. You feel as if you will never recover. Those are very real, factual emotions and circumstances of the moment. But the truth is in such situations that God loves you and will never leave you nor forsake you.[167] He is the friend that sticks closer than a brother.[168] There are hundreds of verses in Scripture that assure us of this truth in such painful moments. You will find that in time, your feelings and perspective have changed as you entrust yourself into the hands of our loving Savior who does the work of healing and comfort.[169]

The only reason that truth exists is because the God of the Bible exists![170] If He doesn't exist, then truth does not exist. This is precisely why the devil has gone to such lengths through liberal theology, liberalism, humanism, Modernism, and Postmodernism, to convince *man* that God doesn't exist or is irrelevant.

---

[166] II Corinthians 4:18

[167] Hebrews 13:5

[168] Proverbs 18:24

[169] Isaiah 41:10; 2 Corinthians 1:3-5

[170] Isaiah 44:6; Psalms 90:2; Malachi 3:6

Just think about this. Truth is so strong that it took the devil nearly 6,000 years just to produce the first substantial fissure in *man's* belief system convincing *him* that God, truth, and absolutes do not exist. Throughout history, there has consistently been more opposition to and hostility towards Biblical, Judeo-Christian faith than against any other belief system or secular non-belief found in the heart of *man*.

The reason for this is simple:

Since the fall of *man* in the Garden of Eden,[171] the devil "owns" everything that is not truth.[172] He is a liar from the beginning and is the father of lies.[173] He hates everything true! Truth is always a threat to the devil because it is a threat to all that is untrue so he works aggressively to destroy every person's acceptance of and confidence in truth. But, his agenda for the eternal destruction of all *mankind* is proven a failure each time someone comes to Christ and is wrested from his grip. Still, he forges ahead, trying to convince the entire human race that God and truth do not exist!

In one way, the greatest success the devil has had over the past two hundred years, from Modernism to Postmodernism, in his war for the soul of *man* is not in convincing *man* that God doesn't exist but rather that the devil himself does not exist!

Keith Green, a Christian artist and prophetic voice in the late '70s until his untimely homegoing in 1982 wrote a song called, *No One Believes in Me Anymore (*aka *Satan's Boast)* describing the cultural and spiritual landscape of that Modern time period. The lyrics are too long to include here but I recommend the reader search for this song and other Keith Green songs for they bear an important message for this generation.

---

[171] Genesis 3

[172] II Corinthians 4:4; Luke 4:5-8

[173] John 8:44

Because God exists, truth exists.[174] And, since truth exists, then truth regarding the condition and moral responsibilities of *mankind* most certainly also exist.

And, since God and truth regarding the responsibilities of *man* exist, then *man* is, by default, accountable to God for that truth.

This is where Biblical Christianity offends Modernism and Postmodernism at the most basic level: in the truth that truth exists and that *man* is accountable to God regarding his moral conduct by extension.

There are three indispensable expressions of Truth. It is only as we embrace these that we will experience true freedom in our life.

1. Jesus Christ: The Personification of Truth

Jesus talked a lot about truth. He told us clearly what and who truth is. He declared emphatically in John 14:6 that He is Truth personified.

> *6 I am the Way, <u>the Truth</u>, and the Life, no man comes to the Father except through Me. (emphasis added)*

Jesus is **the Truth**, not "a truth" as in one of many options or kinds. No, He emphatically declared that He alone is **the Truth**, meaning the only one of its kind. There is no other personification of Truth apart from Jesus.

Jesus did not say of Himself that He knew truth or had truth or contained truth. No, He boldly declared that He Himself is The Truth! No other human being in all of human history is "The Truth." Truth in human form. No one else could qualify. No one else could dare to make such a claim, except the One who truly is Truth… in other words, God Himself. When Jesus walked the earth, He was God in the flesh dwelling among us. Not "a god," but God. Immanuel, God with us.[175]

---

[174] Romans 3:4

[175] John 1:1-3, 12; Isaiah 7:14; Matthew 1:23

Because Jesus Christ is truth in human flesh, He is the key to unlocking the chains of sin and bondage in our lives. He promised that if we will go to Him to be set free... that we will be "free indeed."[176] That simply means that we will be truly and genuinely free from the power and punishment of sin in our life.

Jesus is the only One who can set your spirit and soul free "indeed," permanently and eternally!

There is no genuine freedom for the human soul apart from faith in Christ. None. Period. Every claimed freedom (personal, philosophical, or political) devoid of faith in Christ is superficial, circumstance-based, and temporary. I once had a t-shirt bearing this powerful message:

K**NO**W JESUS, K**NO**W PEACE

Do you see it? If you know Jesus, then you will know and experience peace in your life, but without Him in your life, you will never know or experience genuine peace in your heart and soul.

The words of this song are true:

Only Jesus can satisfy your soul,

Only He can fill your heart and make you whole.

He'll give real peace so deep within,

As He pardons every sin.

Only Jesus can satisfy your soul,

Only Jesus can satisfy your soul.[177]

Postmodernism says you can make or create your own truth and reality but that is a lie. Postmodernism says you can make yourself a boy if you are a girl or vice-versa. That is a lie. It says you can make yourself a better person by yourself but that is also a lie.

---

[176] John 8:36

[177] Words and Music by Karen Cedergren. ©2006 All rights reserved.

Please dear Reader, run to Jesus now if you do not already know Him! He is waiting for you! If you have tried everything else, now it is time to try Jesus.

The Bible extends this invitation to you right now:

> *8 O taste and see that the LORD is good; How blessed is the man who trusts in Him![178]*

Jesus promises that He will never turn away or reject anyone who comes to Him.[179]

2. The Word of God is Truth

Secondly, Jesus, in praying to the Father in John 17:17, made this declaration,

> *17 ...Your Word is truth.*

Psalm 119:160 further declares,

> *160 The entirety of your word is truth... [180]*

So, God's Word, the Holy Bible, is truth. Since truth is immutable, then the Word of God is still true (or truth) today!

Psalms 119:89 says,

> *89 Forever, O Lord, Thy Word is settled in heaven.*

For how long? Forever.

Jesus backed that up in Matthew 24:35 with these words,

> *35 Heaven and earth will pass away, but My words shall not pass away.*

God's Word is Truth. Jesus, who is Truth personified, said so. The Word of God is true whether we believe it, accept it, experience it, understand it, act on it or not! What we do with the Truth (i.e.: God's Word) will not change it but if we will yield to it, it can and will change us, our lives and circumstances.

---

[178] Psalm 34:8

[179] John 6:37

[180] CSB Translation

Jesus made it clear in John 8:32, when He said,

32 You shall know the truth and the truth shall make (or "set") you free. (parenthesis added)

The Word is not true because we experience it… but we may experience it because it is true!

3. Truth in the Life of a Person

Psalm 15:1-2 in the Amplified Bible says,

1 Lord, who shall dwell [temporarily] in Your tabernacle? Who shall dwell [permanently] on Your holy hill? 2 He who walks and lives uprightly and blamelessly, who works rightness and justice and <u>speaks and thinks the truth in his heart</u>.

This is one of the hardest things for any person to do:

To speak and think the truth in his or her heart.

The Psalmist David prayerfully asks, "What does it take to be close to You, Lord, and constantly know Your favor?"

The answer comes to him swiftly in verse two:

1. Walk and live uprightly and blamelessly.

This refers to living with integrity. Integrity means living according to a rigid adherence to a strict code of behavior.

2. Work rightness and justice and,

3. Be able to speak and think *truth* in the heart.

All three prerequisites are tall orders for sure. This is what it takes to live close to God and remain under the cloak of His favor.

Another of the songs the Lord gave me many years ago is entitled, "Greater is the One."[181] The chorus lyrics go like this:

---

[181] Words and Music by Karen Cedergren. ©2004 All rights reserved.

Greater is the One
Who lives in me now.
Now I know the Truth
And the Truth has set me free.
The Truth has set me free.
Oh, greater is the One
Who lives in me now.
I'm living now in truth
And it's truth that keeps me free.
It's truth that keeps me free.

Do you get it? You see, the first half the chorus speaks of coming to know the capital 'T' Truth, the Person of Jesus Christ. He is the only One who can set us free. Once we are set free in Christ, we must learn to live in truth and the truth of God's Word.

The instinct to protect our pride, feelings, and emotions by telling ourselves what we want to hear is part of our frail human nature. In other words, we lie to ourselves. The Bible says when we do this, we are deceiving ourselves and are not allowing *truth* to work in us.[182] We will remain in bondage when we angrily and pridefully defend un-Christlike areas of our character instead of acknowledging and renouncing them. Clinging to lies about ourselves keeps us in bondage. Only in acknowledging the truth, can we begin to be set free.

One of the best promises you can make to yourself is to commit to be honest with yourself, even when it hurts! Perhaps, especially when it hurts.

Don't "kill" the doctor (i.e.: preacher, pastor, counsellor, loved one, or friend) who is delivering to you the medicine you need (i.e.: Word of

---

[182] 1 John 1:6-8

God, truth through preaching or counselling) in order to get rid of an infection (i.e.: un-Christlike character or attitude).[183]

A mother-in-law once told her daughter-in-law, "If the truth is going to hurt my feelings, please tell me a lie." Ouch!

Thinking like that will keep you in spiritual and emotional bondage. Only truth has the power to unlock the chains which bind the heart and soul, painful as it sometimes is to acknowledge. There is no other key that can unlock them.

Feelings of disappointment, failure, condemnation, pride, and inadequacy are merely symptomatic of the real chains that bind up the soul of *man* but Jesus offered this promise and guarantee in John 8:31-32,

> *31 If you hold to my teaching, you are really my disciples.*
> *32 Then you will know the truth, and the truth will set you free. NIV (emphasis added)*

---

[183] Proverbs 9:9-10, 12:15, 23:23, 24:6, 27:5-6; Ephesians 4:25

CHAPTER FOURTEEN

TRADING GOLD FOR BRONZE - A TALE OF THREE GENERATIONS

> *And he took away the treasures of the house of the Lord and the treasures of the king's house, and he took everything; he even took all the shields of gold which Solomon had made. 27 So King Rehoboam made shields of bronze in their place, and entrusted them to the care of the commanders of the guard who guarded the doorway of the king's house.*
>
> *1 Kings 14:26-27*

David's Emphasis: Substance/God (Premodernism)

Let's begin with the obvious. David wasn't perfect.

Only one man in all of human history was perfect, the man, Christ Jesus of Nazareth.[184] Nevertheless, the shepherd boy turned king held a special place in God's heart despite his shortcomings.[185]

What made David so special in the heart of God? What makes him one of the most beloved figures in all the Word of God?

Was it that he was the humble shepherd boy minstrel? Was it because he slew a lion, a bear, and eventually the Philistine giant, Goliath? Was it

---

[184] Isaiah 53:9; 1 Peter 2:22; 2 Corinthians 5:21; Hebrews 4:15; 1 John 3:5
[185] 1 Samuel 13:14; Acts 13:22

his bravery that draws our hearts to him, or perhaps his quick-to-repent nature and forgiving spirit? Was it the fact that even though he had been anointed by God to replace Saul as king over Israel, but did not take the throne by force or insurrection, waiting instead for God to deal with Saul, the point that harnesses the "better angels" in us, as they say?

Most Christians with even a basic knowledge of the story of David would probably agree that it is all of these points and more that endear him to our hearts.

David, the man and his reign over Israel, provide one of the best analogies of the Premodernism in Scripture.

From early childhood to end of life, David was all about truth, substance, conviction... and God: all virtues found in Premodernism. Over and over again throughout his life, David wanted to do the right thing. He wanted to be pleasing to God above all else. When he realized a failure, he sought God's forgiveness and renewed favor.[186] The depth of his desire for fellowship with God is unparalleled in Scripture. No one else brings it home the way David does as he wears his passion for God on his shirtsleeve with beautiful psalms like:

1 As the deer pants for the water brooks, So my soul pants for Thee, O God. Psalm 42:1-2

5 Why, my soul, are you downcast? Why so disturbed within me? Put your hope in God, for I will yet praise him, my Savior and my God. Psalm 42:5,11

11 Teach me Thy way, O Lord; I will walk in Thy truth; Unite my heart to fear Thy name. Psalm 86:11

---

[186] Psalm 32 and 51

23 Search me, O God, and know my heart; Try me and know my anxious thoughts; 24 And see if there be any hurtful way in me, And lead me in the everlasting way. Psalm 139:23-24

Can you feel the pure intent and passion? No wonder we run to David's psalms when we are in distress. No wonder David is called a "man after God's own heart."[187]

David's highest priority was finding a welcome home in the heart of God. Nothing less would do. In every area of life, David pursued God with reckless abandon.[188]

As David established the kingdom for Israel, extending the borders from the time of Saul, the plunder from his defeated foes piled up too. Second Samuel chapter eight records just some of the treasure that David received out of his many military campaign victories. Verse seven says that David brought captured shields of gold to Jerusalem. Solomon might not have become known as the richest man who ever lived, had he not gotten such a good start from the inheritance his father left to him.

All the gold, silver and other precious materials that David secured for Solomon and the building of a future temple remind us that it is our life in Christ and pursuit of His pleasure which are life's true riches today.

Just as David set the tone for his son, Solomon, as to what the kingdom should be like, so Premodernism set the tone for more than 5,500 years for believing in and seeking God. The greatest ever king over Israel laid the groundwork for a kingdom of substance and truth. All Solomon had to do was to keep everything that David put in place going. Solomon's reign would have turned out so differently, if only he had fully heeded his father's parting advice,

---

[187] 1 Samuel 13:14; Acts 13:22
[188] 2 Samuel 6:14, 20-22

9 As for you, my son Solomon, know the God of your father, and serve Him with a whole heart and a willing mind; for the LORD searches all hearts, and understands every intent of the thoughts. If you seek Him, He will let you find Him, but if you forsake Him, He will reject you forever.[189]

You can see that David's final words of advice to Solomon were based on matters of heart and substance. Always seek after and focus on God was the point. If your heart isn't in the right place before God, nothing else will ultimately matter. Show and image will be empty vessels.

David is a picture of Premodernism. By contrast, his son, Solomon, built the temple, wrote thousands of valuable proverbs[190] and then... tossed truth, substance, conviction and God right out the window. Hello Modernism!

Solomon's Focus: Image/Self-Reliance (Modernism)

Is there anything new under the sun?

Apparently not, as Solomon states that there is "nothing new under the sun" (or "under heaven") at least thirty-two times in the Book of Ecclesiastes. Another thirty-three times, he declares, "Vanity of vanities, all is vanity."[191]

The phrase, "vanity of vanities, all is vanity" is written in the Hebrew superlative form, which author, John W. Ritenbaugh, defines this way,

> **That is what Solomon means: Life is absurd. Why do we live? All of our life, we spend working, playing, relating, and at its end, what does a person have to show for what he has done? It is absurd, irrational, meaningless.**[192]

---

[189] 1 Chronicles 28:9

[190] 1 Kings 4:32

[191] Book of Ecclesiastes

[192] bibletools.org

What a perfect description of Modernism.

Some Bible scholars believe that Solomon wrote Ecclesiastes in a backslidden state, in which case we would have to say that this book is the inspired record of some very uninspired utterances of a natural man. Other scholars believe he wrote it after he had returned to the Lord after being backslidden. If that is the case, then Ecclesiastes is the result of a man who was speaking from experience of the futility of a backslidden or sinner's life. Either way, we are rather certain that he wrote this book in his old age. Solomon, at this stage in his life, becomes the consummate example of the following truth:

That the best that man can do on his own, without God, ultimately ends in emptiness for the heart and soul. Without God's blessing: wisdom, position, and riches do not satisfy but only leave one weary and disappointed.

Yet, Solomon did not start out this way.

At the beginning of his life and rulership over Israel, he had looked to God for the help he needed. He asked the Lord to make him wise and God answered his prayer.[193] His dependence on God paid off as the Bible says that he became the wisest man that ever lived.[194]

He inherited a kingdom at peace. Israel had been constantly at war under both Saul and David, but David turned over a strong and stable kingdom at peace to his son. What a blessing for Solomon as he started his reign over Israel.

With the nation at peace for a generation, Solomon had time for other priorities and projects. Periods of immense peace and prosperity in a person's life or that of a nation often lulls the blessed one into a state of complacency. When life is comfortable and luxurious, it is easy to begin to nitpick and focus on matters that are of no eternal significance. In

---

[193] I Kings 3:5-14
[194] I Kings 4:30

prosperity and peace, it is easy for people to begin to indulge in excess. The focus is no longer on substance and matters of real importance in life. The focus becomes self-indulging pleasure and materialism as idle hands become the devil's workshop. What a stark reminder for us to stay focused on and busy with eternal priorities.[195]

Solomon had time to burn because he was not busy defending borders and fighting battles. Time to burn because life came easy for him as his father had done the hard work of subjugating the surrounding nations who were still paying tribute to Israel when Solomon ascended to the throne.

First Kings chapter 10 describes the over-the-top magnitude of Solomon's opulence and wealth.

> *14 Now the weight of gold which came in to Solomon in one year was 666 talents of gold, 15 besides that from the traders and the wares of the merchants and all the kings of the Arabs and the governors of the country. 16 And King Solomon made 200 large shields of beaten gold, using 600 shekels of gold on each large shield. 17 And he made 300 shields of beaten gold, using three minas of gold on each shield, and the king put them [on display] in the house of the forest of Lebanon. 18 Moreover, the king made a great throne of ivory and overlaid it with refined gold. 19 There were six steps to the throne and a round top to the throne at its rear, and arms on each side of the seat, and two lions standing beside the arms. 20 And twelve lions were standing there on the six steps on the one side and on the other; nothing like it was made for any other kingdom. 21 And all King Solomon's drinking vessels were of gold, and all the vessels of the house of the forest of Lebanon were of pure gold. None was of silver; it was not considered valuable in*

---

[195] Luke 2:49; Mark 8:36; Colossians 3:1-3

the days of Solomon. 22 For the king had at sea the ships of Tarshish with the ships of Hiram; once every three years the ships of Tarshish came bringing gold and silver, ivory and apes and peacocks. 23 So King Solomon became greater than all the kings of the earth in riches and in wisdom. 24 And all the earth was seeking the presence of Solomon, to hear his wisdom which God had put in his heart. 25 And they brought every man his gift, articles of silver and gold, garments, weapons, spices, horses, and mules, so much year by year.[196]

Solomon was receiving into his kingdom about 25 tons of gold every year. At today's prices, that's about USD$1.6 billion every year, not including what was coming in from foreign trade routes and so on. With part of this abundance of gold, Solomon made gold shields, placing them in the house of the Forest of Lebanon.

The house of the Forest of Lebanon was part of Solomon's palace. It was much larger than the temple and designed to be a treasury and armory. It got its name from the large amounts of cedar timber used to build it.

These shields made beautiful displays in the house of the Forest of Lebanon, but they were of no use in battle. Gold was too heavy and too soft to be used for shields of war. It was all done to boost and boast of Solomon's image. The opulence was all for show. This is Modernism, the consummate example of "Vanity of vanities; all is vanity."

Fame, power and wealth were his in abundance. The more one has, the more one wants, so Solomon began to want things he shouldn't have. Things that drew his heart away from seeking God as his father, David, had done. Solomon began to think of himself more highly than he ought.[197]

---

[196] 1 Kings 10:14-25 (emphasis added)

[197] Proverbs 3:7; Romans 12:3; Philippians 2:3

It was during his "looking to God" days that Solomon wrote the uplifting Book of Proverbs. Over the years, however, Solomon began to inquire of God less and make his own decisions more. Too bad that he did not hold to the inspired counsel throughout his own life that he recorded for us in Proverbs 3: 5-6,

> *5 Trust in the Lord with all your heart, And lean not on your own understanding; 6 In all your ways acknowledge Him, And He shall direct your paths. (NKJV)*

First Kings 10:26-11:4 describes that the result of his obsession with self-centered, earthly things was that he sinned in four significant areas which led to his fall from the blessing of God on his life.

First of all, he multiplied horses to himself. In other words, he grew his military thus showing that he was depending on his own strength to keep the nation safe rather than depending on God. Remember, he inherited a kingdom at peace. He faced no external threats during his reign. There was no good reason why he needed to increase the size of his military. It was all for image. It was all for show.

Then, he multiplied silver and gold (flooding and thereby ruining the economy, through the devaluation of silver and gold... making these precious metals "common").

He also multiplied wives to himself. Solomon had 700 wives and 300 mistresses (prostitute girlfriends).

Finally, he began to sacrifice to and worship foreign gods. The Bible says that his wives turned his heart away from the Lord. No man's heart could remain faithful to God when ruled by the influence of a thousand women!

Solomon forgot from where God took him. A mistake that his father, David, never made.[198]

---

[198] 1 Kings 11:6,9-13

Still, throughout the book of Ecclesiastes, we find interwoven throughout Solomon's musings on the emptiness of life, his unswerving admission that all human existence without God only leaves the hole in the heart of *man* emptier still.

This is Modernism. Materialism, hedonism, prosperity, progress, and technology offer diversions and a temporary sense of satisfaction, but when all is said and done, nothing and no one, except Jesus Christ, can fill the God-shaped hole in every human heart.

Whereas, the reign and life of David were all about substance and matters of genuine consequence and eternal importance; Solomon's reign, on the other hand, ended up focusing on superficial things like image and self-reliance.

The Book of Ecclesiastes exposes this truth:

That Solomon became more and more "Modernist-like" as the years rolled on, forgetting God and focusing on *man* as the center of the universe.

Rehoboam's Reign: Just Pure Chaos (Postmodernism)

Solomon inherited a kingdom at peace and well provided for from his father, David. Rehoboam inherited a kingdom of gold from his father, Solomon. He traded it for bronze and lost the kingdom in just five years' time. In other words, Rehoboam inherited Modernism and then ran with it right into Postmodernism. Because of Solomon's sin and Rehoboam's foolishness, the united kingdom Rehoboam received descended into Postmodern-like chaos and split into two.[199]

But how did Rehoboam lose it all?

Unfortunately, Rehoboam did not inherit the wisdom that his father, Solomon, had early in life. He started his reign over the nation with foolish decisions instead.[200]

---

[199] 1 Kings 14:30
[200] 1 Kings 12:1-15

Rehoboam went all-out Emergent! (Remember that term from chapter six?)

The people came to him, asking him to lighten the burden of their forced labor so he told them to wait three days for his answer.

First, he consulted with counsellors from his father's generation; elders who had served under his father.

Here is that part of the story:

> *6 And King Rehoboam consulted with the <u>elders who had served his father Solomon</u> while he was still alive, saying, "How do you advise me to answer this people?" 7 Then they spoke to him, saying, "If you will be a servant to this people today, and will serve them and grant them their request, and speak pleasant words to them, then they will be your servants always.[201]*

Let's read on...

> *8 But he <u>ignored the advice of the elders</u> which they had given him, and <u>consulted with the young men who had grown up with him and served him</u>. 9 He said to them, "What advice do you give, so that we may answer this people who have spoken to me, saying, 'Lighten the yoke which your father put on us'?" 10 And the young men who had grown up with him spoke to him, saying, "This is what you should say to this people who spoke to you, saying: 'Your father made our yoke heavy, now you make it lighter for us!' You should speak this way to them: 'My little finger is thicker than my father's waist! 11 Now then, my father loaded you with a heavy yoke; yet I will add to your yoke. My father disciplined you with whips, but I will discipline you with*

---

[201] 1 Kings 12:6-7 (emphasis added)

scorpions!'" 12 Then Jeroboam and all the people came to Rehoboam on the third day, just as the king had directed, saying, "Return to me on the third day." 13 And the king answered the people harshly, for he ignored the advice of the elders which they had given him, 14 and he spoke to them according to the advice of the young men, saying, "My father made your yoke heavy, but I will add to your yoke; my father disciplined you with whips, but I will discipline you with scorpions!" [202]

Churches and ministries benefit greatly from the youthful zeal, freshness, and energy that young people bring. That is a no brainer. But young people still need and can benefit from the older generation who have more life experience and wisdom to draw from too. All generations have assets to offer God's Kingdom. All are valuable.

Using my own life as an example, I am absolutely in favor of tapping youthful zeal and gifts in ministry. I started in Christian missions on my own at the age of 19. At 22 years old, I was cofounding a Bible School in the Philippines together with my parents. I brought some gift assets to the table, and they brought wisdom and other gifts to the table. I benefited from working with my parents who were in their early 50s when we started the Bible School. They benefited from my youthful zeal, but to tell you the truth, they stood a better chance of pioneering a Bible School without me than I did without them. Praise God, He put our multi-generational team together to accomplish the Call!

Rehoboam dismissed the reasoned counsel of the elders and embraced the foolish advice of his generational contemporaries.

---

[202] 1 Kings 12:8-13 (emphasis added)

News flash! This is how Emergent mindset works under Postmodernism. Remember? Out with the old, in with only the young and inexperienced generation. Only those who are considered young enough are desired, relevant, and worth keeping around. Youthful zeal is more important. Life experience and the wisdom that normally comes with age need not apply.

Within five very short years, Postmodern Rehoboam wrecked the kingdom he had received. A very important part of the story of Rehoboam is found in 1 Kings 14:25-27 (emphasis added),

> *25 Now it happened in the fifth year of King Rehoboam, that Shishak the king of Egypt marched against Jerusalem. 26 And <u>he took away the treasures</u> of the house of the Lord <u>and the treasures</u> of the king's house, and <u>he took</u> <u>everything; he even took all the shields of gold which</u> Solomon <u>had made.</u> 27 <u>So King Rehoboam made shields</u> <u>of bronze in their place,</u> and entrusted them to the care of the commanders of the guard who guarded the doorway of the king's house. 28 And it happened as often as the king entered the house of the Lord, that the guards would carry them and would bring them back into the guards' room.*

Rehoboam thought he could do whatever he wanted with no accountability to God. He was wrong. The Lord removed His hand of protection and allowed the king of Egypt to invade. The Egyptian king took the wealth of the national treasury along with the shields of gold accumulated during the administrations of both David and Solomon.

Rehoboam decided he could fix the problem by replacing them with shields made from bronze (or brass). Rehoboam didn't care about what God thought of him. He was too deep into himself and his Postmodern mindset to care. All that mattered to him was that he still had some shiny shields that he could bring out and put on display when he wanted make an impression.

There is a big difference between gold and brass. Brass tarnishes and is not worth nearly as much as gold. Ask any Olympian who won a gold medal if they would trade their medal for a bronze medal instead.

The answer will come back to you stinging, "No way! Are you kidding?"

All this is an example of the emphasis of image over substance that began in the days of Solomon (Modern) and worsened under Rehoboam (Postmodern). Because all they were interested in was image, the substance of David's (Premodern) world was lost and carried away.

Rehoboam's sin turned a golden kingdom into bronze. The dynasty of David went from gold to bronze in just five years.

Second Chronicles 12:14 summarizes Rehoboam's life and reign like this,

> *14 And he did evil, because he did not prepare his heart to seek the Lord.*

This speaks to the lack of his personal relationship with the Lord, a sure way to go from gold to bronze.

The gold shields were handed over to Shishak, the king of Egypt in an attempt to appease him. It is significant that it was the king of Egypt which carted off with the gold shields that David and Solomon had added to the national treasury. Egypt is a type of Satan's kingdom, the unregenerate life, and the world's system in Scripture.

Postmodernism is Rehoboam's chaotic, gold-for-bronze trade-off kingdom playing out all over again! I pray for every church or minister that is following Rehoboam's style of leadership (i.e.: Postmodern fads, trends, styles, and fashions) instead of sticking to the model that David gave us.

How often do we, as God's people, trade away gold for bronze? Postmodern culture will surely put pressure on you to give up your gold (i.e.: your faith, your testimony, your convictions, holy living, your life in Christ, etc.) but, like the gold-medalist Olympian, with our life firmly planted in Christ, we must also shout resoundingly, "No way! Are you kidding?"

When churches rely on activities and programs to be the "anointing" that draws and keeps people rather than the pastor and the church themselves doing the hard work in prayer on bended knee for anointed preaching and teaching, we are trading gold for bronze.

When churches rely on material things such as Postmodern sanctuary appearances outfitted with the most modern accessories and only the most talented singers to lead musically to be the criteria by which we gage our church's worth and success, we are trading gold for bronze.

When we neglect our eternal purpose for temporal desire, pleasure, and entertainment, we are trading gold for bronze.

We are robbed of spiritual strength and intimacy with God every time we sin or compromise and then work so hard to keep up an outward appearance of spiritual health through sheer busy-ness for Him. This, too, is trading gold for bronze.

When ritual replaces relationship we are trading gold for bronze.[203]

When we begin to serve God on autopilot instead of from deep love and devotion, we are trading gold for bronze.[204]

In going to the cross instead of running from it, Jesus became our greatest example of holding onto His gold and not trading it off for bronze.[205] Jesus could have taken the easy way out by requesting the Father to dispatch twelve legions of angels to rescue him in that moment, but He did not do that, praise God.[206]

If the emphasis of the believer individually, the local church, or the great universal Body of Christ is forever on shiny brass substitutes then we are in trouble.

---

[203] Mark 7:1-13

[204] Hebrews 11:24-26

[205] Isaiah 50:7; Luke 9:51

[206] Matthew 26:53

If we need high tech trappings or the coolest, hippest, famous preacher in front of us or on our mobile device to make our "doing church" worthwhile, then we are in trouble, for this is the very essence of the truth found in 2 Timothy 3:5,

> *holding to a form of godliness although they have denied its power; avoid such people as these.*

Contrariwise, Isaiah 60:16-18 issues this wonderful promise to all who would pursue the Lord with the abandon of David:

> *16 Powerful kings and mighty nations shall provide you with the choicest of their goods to satisfy your every need, and you will know at last and really understand that I, the Lord, am your Savior and Redeemer, the Mighty One of Israel. 17 I will exchange your brass for gold, your iron for silver, your wood for brass, your stones for iron. Peace and righteousness shall be your taskmasters! 18 Violence will disappear out of your land—all war will end. Your walls will be 'Salvation' and your gates 'Praise.'*[207]

Christian, keep your gold!

---

[207] Isaiah 60:16-18 TLB (emphasis added)

CHAPTER FIFTEEN

LESSONS FROM CHURCH HISTORY

For I will show you lessons from our history, stories
handed down to us from former generations. 4 I will
reveal these truths to you so that you can describe these
glorious deeds of Jehovah to your children and tell them
about the mighty miracles He did.
Psalm 78:2-4 TLB

As we continue to dive deeper into the solutions end of this book, another model we can look to for guidance on how to navigate through this Postmodern world, is church history. Church history offers us valuable lessons to live by if we have an open heart to receive them.

There is a famous saying which says that those who do not learn the lessons of history (i.e.: the mistakes) are bound or destined to repeat them. The same holds true for church history. The lessons of church history are applicable to the believer individually, the local church uniquely, and the Body of Christ in general, across every epoch of time. Failure to heed the lessons only results in the Church making the same mistakes over and over again while completely missing the guidance.

Here are just a few of the most compelling lessons from church history, providing a road map for the believer, the local church, and the Body of Christ in general, in navigating Postmodern life today. How did the Church conduct itself in the midst of the culture and world around them throughout church history?

The following lessons are derived from looking at both what the Church did right and where it went wrong along the way. Let's go!

Religion is man's effort to justify himself before God. True Biblical Christianity is not religion, nor a religion, but rather a living relationship with Jesus Christ.

Postmodernism is full of religions and philosophies, all of which are devoid of the power to make right one's standing before God.

All the "isms" in the world are acceptable to Postmodernism: Modernism, Postmodernism, Deism, Docetism, Heathenism, Humanism, Islamism, Buddhism, Hinduism, Bahaism, Shamanism, Shintoism, Individualism, Animism, Atheism, Agnosticism, Anti-Semitism, Communism, Secularism, Materialism, Gnosticism, Sexism, Anarchism, Amoralism, Socialism, Extremism, Activism, and even Catholicism and religious Protestantism, and so on…

So many "isms" and Postmodernism adds more all the time!

All these are welcome in Postmodernism because all of them lead people away from the Truth. That is why they are welcome.

But notice the unique identification of these two words: Christianity and Christendom. You see, there is no "ism" in real Biblical Christianity. Postmodern Christians integrate "isms" into their faith and worldview. Bible-based believers must reject them.

Churches, ministries, organizations, and denominational labels cannot save anyone. There is no salvation in the name of your church or mine. The Bible clearly says in Acts 4:12,

12 And there is salvation in <u>no one</u> else; for there is <u>no other name</u> under heaven that has been given among men by which we must be saved. (emphasis added)

The name and person referenced here which have the exclusive power to save is the Lord Jesus Christ of Nazareth.

God has no grandchildren, only children.

Religion cannot save you or make you right before God, not even nominal, ceremonial, religious Christianity. Not church membership or infant baptism or teenage Confirmation. Apart from a living and personal relationship with Jesus Christ, all one is left with in life is an "ism."

Perhaps, you are hoping in "trusting-in-self-ism"[208] or "being-a-good-person-ism" or "good-works-ism" to save you, but these cannot bring you to heaven. You must be born again.[209]

The Church has always had its greatest impact on the world when it is *least* like the world; Always more powerful and fruitful for the Gospel when clean![210]

When God called the nation of Israel into existence in the Old Testament, His intention was for them to be unique, distinct from the world around them, and exclusively His.[211] And, there were periods of time throughout Israel's history when, through a godly leader and national repentance, they did walk in this Calling for a time; however, for most of Israel's history, they craved to be like the world around them. Their craving led them to compromise, and that compromise diluted the impact of their testimony to the world.[212]

---

[208] Proverbs 3:5-6, 28:26; Ezekiel 33:13; Isaiah 64:6; Luke 18:9; 2 Corinthians 1:9

[209] John 3:3-7; Ephesians 2:8-9; Titus 3:5

[210] 2 Corinthians 3:18, 4:8-11, 6:17-18; 2 Timothy 3:12; Matthew 5:10-12

[211] Deuteronomy 7:6-8, 14:1; 1 Kings 8:53

[212] 1 Samuel chapter 8; 1 Corinthians 10:1-12

And so it is with all who belong to God.

From the inception of the Church in the Book of Acts, persecution has been a companion of genuine Christianity. For the first forty years, persecution came against the Church from religious Judaism. After the Fall of Jerusalem in 70AD until 313AD, the Roman Empire breathed the heaviest threats against the Church. Then, for the next 1,200 years, the true Church of Jesus Christ was most severely persecuted by the religious, institutional machine called the Roman Catholic Church.

One of the distinct results or effects that persecution had on the Church during the Persecuted Church Age (100AD – 313AD) in church history was that the Church became a purified Church. Persecution kept away all who were insincere in their profession of faith. No one joined the Church for worldly gain or popularity. Unfortunately, Western Postmodern Christianity is full of eager stars today.

History of the Christian Church writes of this time,

> **The long and bloody war of heathen Rome against the church, which is built upon a rock, utterly failed. It began in Rome under Nero, it ended near Rome at the Milvian bridge, under Constantine. Aiming to exterminate, [instead] it purified.**[213]

In one way, Christians almost welcomed persecution, wearing it as a badge of honor. Persecution is what separated true followers of Jesus Christ from everyone else. There were no religious, insincere, or ill-motivated "Christians" in that atmosphere of intense persecution.

The courage of Christians stunned the spectators in coliseums time and time again as they faced the cruelest forms of martyrdom. They were thrown to the lions, burned at the stake, stoned, crucified, beheaded, sawn in two, sown into gutted bear skins and left to flounder until they expired, and other forms of cruel death.

---

[213] ccel.org (brackets added)

One of the original twelve Apostles, Missionary Bartholomew, was flayed alive in a foreign land as a result of his successful preaching because of the great number of people who came to believe in Christ.

Tertullian, who was one of the main church leaders of that period, wrote this famous quote regarding the persecution, *"The blood of the martyrs is the seed of the Church."*

In every way that counts, the Church behaved nothing like the world and the world took notice. The courage and conviction seen in the Christians throughout that time period was the testimony that caused even more to believe.

Would the following testimony from the second century Church also as aptly describe today's Postmodern Church? Think about it.

"Those Christians" is a letter that was written and circulated during the second century. You can sense the awe and respect held by the anonymous author for these second century followers of Christ.

> **For the Christians are not differentiated from other people by country, language or customs; you see they do not live in cities of their own, or speak some strange dialect, or have some peculiar lifestyle.**
>
> **This teaching of theirs has not been contrived by the invention and speculation of inquisitive men; nor are they propagating mere human teaching as some people do. They live in both Greek and foreign cities, wherever chance has put them. They follow local customs in clothing, food and the other aspects of life. But at the same time, they demonstrate to us the wonderful and certainly unusual form of their own citizenship.**
>
> **They live in their own native lands, but as aliens; as citizens, they share all things with others; but like aliens, suffer all things. Every foreign country is to them as their native country, and every native land as a foreign country.**

They marry and have children just like everyone else; but they do not kill unwanted babies. They offer a shared table, but not shared bed. They are at present 'in the flesh' but they do not live 'according to the flesh'. They are passing their days on earth, but are citizens of heaven. They obey the appointed laws, and go beyond the laws in their own lives.

They love everyone, but are persecuted by all. They are unknown and condemned; they are put to death and gain life. They are poor and yet make many rich. They are short of everything and yet have plenty of all things. They are dishonoured and yet gain glory through dishonour.

Their names are blackened and yet they are cleared. They are mocked and bless in return. They are treated outrageously and behave respectfully to others. When they do good, they are punished as evildoers; when punished, they rejoice as if being given new life. They are attacked by Jews as aliens, and are persecuted by Greeks; yet those who hate them cannot give any reason for their hostility.

To put it simply -- the soul is to the body as Christians are to the world. The soul is spread through all parts of the body and Christians through all the cities of the world. The soul is in the body but is not of the body; Christians are in the world but not of the world.[214]

Wow! What a powerful commendation of the reputation the second century Church held before the world around them. How about the Western Church today? Would the same be said of it?

---

[214] Lion Handbook: The History of Christianity, p. 67

The description in this second century letter is consistent with everything we learn in the New Testament about how we are to embrace our faith in Jesus, but it does not well describe the present testimony of Postmodern Christianity today. What a sad thing to have to write. Way too many Postmodern Christians are so busy with their feelings, their need for constant affirmation, comfort and ease, and their insatiable hunger for entertainment.

The Church and the individual believer need not seek for persecution, but we also must not choose compromise, acquiescing to the world, in order to avoid it when it does come.

Persecution is not a message that Christians want to hear. Sadly, many Christians have convinced themselves that they are so special to God that they will never experience real persecution. They have found a way to explain away how persecution was for the true Church in church history and for modern-day believers in other countries, but not for the Church in the West.

The fact is that true believers of Jesus Christ have suffered persecution since the inception of the Church. It is not a novel phenomenon. Statistics reveal that more followers of Jesus Christ around the globe were martyred for their faith in the twentieth century alone more than all nineteen centuries that preceded it.[215]

The Church, especially the Western Church, must heed the wake-up call in this 21st century as it begins to feel the heat of rejection from all sectors of society.

The following are excerpts from a letter from the famous Corrie ten Boom, written in 1974 from China to the American church. It contains important counsel on how to prepare for persecution:

---

[215] christianity.com/church/church-history/timeline/1901-2000/modern-persecution-11630665

My sister, Betsy, and I were in the Nazi concentration camp at Ravensbruck because we committed the crime of loving Jews. Seven hundred of us from Holland, France, Russia, Poland and Belgium were herded into a room built for two hundred. As far as I knew, Betsy and I were the only two representatives of Heaven in that room.

We may have been the Lord's only representatives in that place of hatred, yet because of our presence there, things changed. Jesus said, "In the world you shall have tribulation; but be of good cheer, I have overcome the world." We too, are to be overcomers – bringing the light of Jesus into a world filled with darkness and hate...

How can we get ready for the persecution?

First we need to feed on the Word of God, digest it, make it a part of our being. This will mean disciplined Bible study each day as we not only memorize long passages of scripture, but put the principles to work in our lives.

Next we need to develop a personal relationship with Jesus Christ. Not just the Jesus of yesterday, the Jesus of History, but the life-changing Jesus of today who is still alive and sitting at the right hand of God.

We must be filled with the Holy Spirit. This is no optional command of the Bible, it is absolutely necessary. Those earthly disciples could never have stood up under the persecution of the Jews and Romans had they not waited for Pentecost. Each of us needs our own personal Pentecost, the baptism of the Holy Spirit. We will never be able to stand in tribulation without it.

In the coming persecution we must be ready to help each other and encourage each other. But we must not wait until... tribulation comes before starting. The fruit of the

Spirit should be the dominant force of every Christian's life.

Many are fearful of coming tribulation, they want to run. I, too, am a little bit afraid when I think that after all my eighty years, including the horrible Nazi concentration camp, that I might have to go through [more] tribulation also. But then I read the Bible and I am glad.

When I am weak, then I shall be strong, the Bible says. Betsy and I were prisoners for the Lord, we were so weak, but we got power because the Holy Spirit was on us. That mighty inner strengthening of the Holy Spirit helped us through. No, you will not be strong in yourself when tribulation comes. Rather, you will be strong in the power of Him who will not forsake you. For seventy-six years I have known the Lord Jesus and not once has He ever left me or let me down.

"Though He slay me, yet will I trust Him," (Job 13:15) for I know that to all who overcome, He shall give the crown of life. Hallelujah!" - Corrie Ten Boom – 1974 [216]

The comfortable Church in the comfortable West may one day be comfortable no more. Postmodernism is a primary tool in the hands of the devil that is hastening the dawning of that day.

Pastors must begin to prepare the sheep to cling to Christ as we see that day approaching.[217]

I once gave my brother a Christian poster for his birthday. It was a photo of a lone guy in a kayak trying to stay upright while negotiating a violent set of river rapids. The photo perfectly captured the danger the

---

[216] Brackets have been added to help clarify context.
[217] Ephesians 5:11-17, Romans 13:11-12

kayaker was facing with the water in the still shot erupting everywhere in the scene, smashing into the kayak and surrounding boulders.

The caption at the bottom of the poster delivered this promise,

"God never promised us an easy ride… only a safe landing."

Believer, you have two choices in life: dive deeply into Christ and find safety or drown in the waters of Postmodernism.

The Church gets in trouble when it conflates patriotism with Christianity.

God wanted Israel to be a theocracy in the Old Testament. He wanted them to look to Him as their king. Well, they blew it and demanded a flesh and blood king that they could see with their eyes. They wanted to be like the nations around them.[218]

From 313AD until the Reformation of the Church in the 16th century, the Roman version of Christianity dominated every facet of life and government in Europe and everywhere else Roman Catholic explorers colonized. There was some good and a lot of bad as a result. The bad included 1,000 years of "The Dark Ages" from the 5th century until the 14th century.

Also included in the bad was the Inquisition which was a Catholic Church led court imposed all over Europe for the purpose of squelching anyone and everyone who did not tow the Catholic line. The Inquisition's methods employed to achieve this goal were the cruelest, most brutal and inhumane forms of torture and death… all done in the name of Christ. The Inquisition was not employed against pagans, Muslims, or Jews. Its target group were those who called themselves Christians but did not bow to the doctrines of the Roman Church. Here is the lesson for us:

It is never a good thing for a nation when a religion controls the levers of power, any religion… Sorry, saints, but not even when it is religious Christianity. Flawed men and women are simply incapable of faithfully

---

[218] Judges 8:23; Deuteronomy 17:14-20; 1 Samuel chapter 8

wielding such power, especially in the name of religion, without falling into abuses of every kind.

Although Biblical theocracy is the ideal, it is not going to happen until King Jesus sets up His Millennial government. Until then, Biblical theocracy can only take place spiritually, on an individual basis, as believers submit to the rulership of the Lord Jesus Christ and His Kingdom over their lives.

Many Christians try so hard to hold tightly to the idea of God ruling through the secular government of their nation that they conflate the two exclusively unique forms of government, democracy and Biblical theocracy, in the name of patriotism.

Although democracy suffers from many flaws and has no place in the Kingdom of God, it does serve as the best governmental system a nation can hope for when influenced by Judeo-Christian principles but not ruled theocratically until Jesus comes again. I have been to Israel multiple times and love this Holy Land nation; however, theocracy doesn't even work there. The modern-day nation of Israel is governed by democracy just like all other democratic nations.

The founders of Switzerland (1291) and the USA (1776) got it right when they wrote into their rule-by-the-people-based Constitutions the "freedom of religion" and the "separation of church and state." God bless Christians who run for political office, but the Church must never lose sight of its highest responsibilities in every society, which are prayer and light shining through believers individually and through the local church collectively, not the politicization of the Church.

We know that in the Millennium, King Jesus will rule undisputed, but until that day comes, the reality is that the closer we come to the end of the age, the more evil human government will become, not the more godly.

Christians must never idolize a nation. Our heart, highest loyalty, and priority must remain where our eternal citizenship lies, in heaven![219] It will

---

[219] Philippians 3:20; 1 Chronicles 7:14; Acts chapters 4-5; 4:13, 17:6; 1 Chronicles 29:15; Psalm 39:12; Psalm 119:19; Psalm 119:54; Hebrews 11:9; Hebrews 11:13

be imperative in the days to come that believers remain more loyal to their heavenly citizenship over that of any on earth.

Let's endeavor to live up to the testimony left to us as described in the anonymous letter, *"Those Christians."*

Paganism in the name of Christianity is far more dangerous and deadly than outright paganism!

29 The Lord your God will destroy the nations where you're going and force them out of your way. You will take possession of their land and live there. 30 After they've been destroyed, be careful you aren't tempted to follow their customs. Don't even ask about their gods and say, 'How did these people worship their gods? We want to do what they did.'[220]

Paganism is a catch-all term that refers to all forms of religious belief and practice not based on the God of the Bible.

Not since before the Reformation of the Church in the 16th century has there been such an influx of paganism adapted into the practice of the Christian faith as Postmodern Christianity welcome elements of New Age thought and Eastern religions into its belief system and worldview.

When the Roman Emperor, Constantine, issued the Edict of Toleration over the empire in 313AD, everything became so much easier for the Church. In the new atmosphere of peace and comfort, compromise flourished. It became popular to join the church without being truly saved. The masses began to join Christianity as one would join a social club. As a consequence, they brought their pagan customs with them into their new club membership.

For the next 1,200 years, a religious machine called "Christianity," dominated by Catholicism, spread throughout Europe. Internally, it was

---

[220] Deuteronomy 12:29-30 GOD's WORD Translation (emphasis added)

filled with sin, hypocrisy, politics and power brokers, and pagan practices touched up with Bible verses... but very little light. Christianity was institutionalized.

Paganism in the name of Christianity is dangerous. We are witnessing it in the Postmodern practice of the Christian life.

Christianity's greatest enemy is conformity to the world (it's system and mindset).

This point was well discussed in chapters six and seven, especially as it relates to the world's influence on church forms and culture.

Here, we want to look more specifically as it relates to the influence of the world on the individual believer.

The Bible tells us not to be conformed to this world.[221]

The word, *conformed*, means

> **to fashion or shape one thing like another... The verb has more especial reference to that which is transitory, changeable, unstable... [The Greek word] could not be used of inward transformation.**[222]

It means to make one thing into the mold of another. Don't allow yourself to be squeezed into the mold of culture around you.

The commentary on Romans 12:2 in the New Living Translation Study Bible explains "conformed" this way,

> **Paul warned Christians, 'Don't copy the behavior and customs of this world," which is selfish and corrupting. Many Christians wisely decide that a large portion of the world's behavior is off-limits for them. Our refusal to conform to this world, however, must go even deeper than just behavior and customs – it must be firmly planted in the values rooted**

---

[221] Romans 12:2

[222] Vine's Complete Expository Dictionary of New Testament Words (emphasis and brackets added)

in our mind: 'Let God transform you into a new person by changing the way you think.' It is possible to avoid most worldly customs and still be proud, covetous, selfish, stubborn, and arrogant. Only when the Holy Spirit renews, reeducates, and redirects our mind are we truly transformed.

The Bible warns us not to love the world, and neither to conform to its ways. Doing so makes us an enemy of God and demonstrates that God's love is not at work in our life.[223]

This means more than just not drinking, smoking, or watching bad movies. Our thought life, values, priorities, and affections must not be conformed to that of the world around us.

The interests of the child of God are to be focused on things above, not on the things of the earth.[224]

Too many Christians want their "ticket" to heaven secured for the future while insisting on their "right" to enjoy a kind of moral and behavioral "license" in the present. True Biblical Christianity doesn't work like that. Christ calls us to live for Him now.[225]

20 For I have been crucified with Christ; and it is no longer I who live, but Christ lives in me; and the life which I now live in the flesh I live by faith in the Son of God, who loved me, and delivered Himself up for me.[226]

14 But may it never be that I should boast, except in the cross of our Lord Jesus Christ, through which the world has been crucified to me, and I to the world.[227]

---

[223] James 4:4; 1 John 2:15-17

[224] Colossians 3:1-3

[225] 2 Corinthians 6:2; Ecclesiastes 12:1; Galatians 6:7-8

[226] Galatians 2:20

[227] Galatians 6:14

What more can be said? Nothing more is needed.

True movements of God are based on points of doctrine and moves of the Spirit marked by healings and miracles that draw the lost to repentance and impact cities and nations, not ever-changing cultural trends, ministry styles and methods!
Let's not conflate passing, culture-based styles, trends, hype, fads, and fashions with spiritual moves of God. They are not the same.

In Ephesians 4:13-14, we read that we are supposed to grow up into mature Christians who are no longer,

> *14 tossed back and forth [like ships on a stormy sea] and carried about by every wind of [shifting] doctrine, by the cunning and trickery of [unscrupulous] men, by the deceitful scheming of people ready to do anything [for personal profit]. (Amplified Bible)*

Church cultural styles, trends, hype, fads and fashions come and go! They change. Don't follow them around as if they were some mighty move of God, dear saint in Christ!

> *26 Watch the path of your feet And all your ways will be established.[228]*

In Philippians 4:11-13, Paul talks about being content in whatever circumstance of life he found himself in. The word, *content*, means "to be independent of the circumstances."

The notes in the NLT Study Bible on these verses shed light on what Paul is saying,

---

[228] Proverbs 4:26

Paul could get along happily because he could see life from God's point of view. He focused on what he was supposed to do, not what he felt he should have. Paul had his priorities straight, and he was grateful for everything God had given him. Paul had detached himself from the nonessentials so that he could concentrate on the eternal.

Live out your faith independent of and above the din of culture. Hold to a practice of faith which doesn't need to change again and again as the whims of culture change.

That means rain or shine, rich or barely having enough, famous or unknown, single or married, children or none, well-liked or set aside, at the top of our profession or merely a humble laborer, when the storms of life push and pull or we are sailing along on still, glassy water... sweet contentment and stability of faith will be ours as this beautiful hymn describes.

My hope is built on nothing less
Than Jesus blood and righteousness;
I dare not trust the sweetest frame,
But wholly lean on Jesus' name.

On Christ, the solid Rock, I stand;
All other ground is sinking sand.

When darkness veils His lovely face,
I rest on His unchanging grace;
In every high and stormy gale,
My anchor holds within the veil.

His oath, His covenant, His blood,
Support me in the whelming flood;

When all around my soul gives way,
He then is all my hope and stay.

When He shall come with trumpet sound,
Oh, may I then in Him be found;
In Him, my righteousness, alone,
Faultless to stand before the throne.[229]

When our faith is anchored in Christ, we shall indeed sing with all our heart, "It is well, it is well with my soul."[230]

God wants us *insulated* from the world, not isolated from it!
In Greece, there is a famous rocky cliff formation called the Meteora. Wikipedia says of this place,

> **The Meteora is a rock formation in central Greece hosting one of the largest and most precipitously built complexes of Eastern Orthodox monasteries, second in importance only to Mount Athos. The six monasteries [of an original twenty-four] are built on immense natural pillars and hill-like rounded boulders that dominate the local area.[231]**

I had the privilege of leading a group from our church there. It was an amazing experience. It is so impressive how the monks of old built these monasteries in the 14th and 15th centuries at the top or right into the side of rock pillars and cliffs with terrifying vertical drops of 1,900 feet (600 meters) or more.

---

[229] On Christ the Solid Rock I Stand; Music by John Bacchus Dykes (1823-76), Lyrics by
[230] Edward Mote (1787-1874)
[231] It Is Well; Lyrics by Horatio Spafford (1828-1888), Music by Philip Bliss (1838-1876)
  wikipedia.org/wiki/Meteora (brackets added)

As the centuries after Christ wore on, a trend developed among men who wanted to remain undefiled from the world around them. They thought the best way to do this was to *isolate* themselves completely from society. This system became known as Monasticism. Another "ism"...

> **Monasticism is essentially seclusion from the world for religious purposes and usually involves ascetic practices to some degree. The beginning of monasticism in the Church is traced to Anthony (b. 250) in Egypt. In his youth he sold his possessions, and went into solitude, engaging in prayer and the strictest self-denial. A certain Pachomius supposedly improved monasticism by establishing the first monasteries.[232]**

Remember the quote about the second century Christians earlier in this chapter? Notice that although they were the outsiders of society, they did not seclude themselves away. They were, as God intends for us to be, passing through this world without becoming stained by the spirit and mindset of it.[233] They were living as testimonies of God's grace and power in the midst of an evil generation, not hidden away but as a city set on a hill.[234]

I grew up in a small town in Minnesota and went to public school my whole childhood. The theory of evolution was about the worst thing I can remember being taught as I grew up under Modernism. What children are taught today in public schools all over the world is a million times worse.

We can understand why parents choose to homeschool their own children or enroll them in private Christian schools when possible. For much of the world, however, homeschooling, and private Christian schools

---

[232] bible.ca

[233] James 1:27

[234] Matthew 5:14-16

are not available or simply not an option. For example, homeschooling is not available in Switzerland. In this case, Christian parents must then have one all-encompassing goal: to arm and **insulate** their child(ren) to be shining lights for Christ in their public school systems by instilling the fear of the Lord in them. By the phrase, "the fear of the Lord," I am talking about the following:

• Developing a wholesome, healthy dread of displeasing God. In order for a child to have a healthy desire not to displease God, he or she need a wholesome respect for how Mom and Dad are living before them at home as a role model.

"I am disappointed with you," were the words that I did not want to hear my parents say when I was a teenager for they were a far more effective form of discipline than any spanking on my seat of education!

When my late brother, Alan, was about 30 years old and married, he once asked me, "Karen, did you ever try drinking or smoking and stuff like that when you were in high school?"

"No Al, not even once," was my quick reply, "how about you?"

"I didn't dare," he shot back, "I didn't want to disappoint Mom and Dad."

"Me too, Al, me too."

You see, the respect we held for our parents produced in us a healthy dread of displeasing them. That loving respect combined together with the relationship we each had individually with Jesus kept us on the straight and narrow throughout our teenage years and became our lifelong lifestyle. We both knew that if we ever had decided to experiment with drinking, smoking, or drugs, or give way to rage and uncontrolled anger, lying, cheating, living a double life, etc. that we could never point a finger at either of our parents and say, "We saw this in you and learned this from you."

A few years ago, I invited a couple who are pastors and friends of mine to guest speak in our church retreat. The pastor and his wife had raised four children, all of whom stayed with the Lord throughout their youth and into adulthood. As adults, all four children are serving in church ministry together with their own families. To God be the glory for such a wonderful result! I believe that God honored their sincere efforts in both pastoring the church they founded and in being godly examples to their children. It was what he said about the commitment he made to himself that caught my attention.

He said, "If my children saw me mess up with a bad attitude or unkind words, etc. towards them or others while they were growing up, I made sure that they also saw me repent, ask forgiveness, and make it right."

Praise God! No wonder his children grew up with a healthy view of Christianity and church ministry. It makes the challenge of staying undefiled by the world so much easier for children when they have confidence that their parents, especially their dads, are living humble, godly lives with few contradictions and no hypocrisy. No, "Do as I say, but not as I do," lifestyle.[235]

• Discipline of children must be grounded in the love and Word of God and consistent with the claims of parents regarding their faith.

It is self-defeating when Christian parents discipline their children using the methods and standards of the world. On every level of life, Christian discipline must be based on and applied through the lens of the Word and love of God. If parents bring their children to church and then exclude God, His Word, and prayer from the correction process at home, the child will grow up with a conflicted and compartmentalized view of Christianity.

Obviously, disciplinary methods differ depending on the age of the child, but here are some basics:[236]

---

[235] Deuteronomy 6:2,6-7,20-25; Psalm 78:1-7; 1 Corinthians 11:1
[236] Hebrews 12:5-13; Proverbs 3:11-12, 13:24

1. What does God's Word say about the disobedient act? Take the time to explain your heart to the child through the use of God's Word. This helps to establish His Word as the authority over their life and behavior. Prayer also helps to soften the heart.

2. Never take out on a child, in the name of discipline, the anger and frustration you are dealing with in other areas of your own personal life. God did not give that child to you to be your punching bag, unloading on them the fury of your anger and frustration from other areas of your life, for things they did not do. This happens all too often with parents unfortunately.

3. Slapping a child on the face, beating a child, unleashing rage and threats will never produce the wholesome fear of the Lord in that child and will probably result in that child hating God rather than drawing closer to Him. Correction and disciplinary methods which humiliate, berate, and condemn are never representative of the heart of God.

4. Unbelievable as it may sound, some Christian parents use their child's love for God and church as a disciplinary weapon over them by telling the child that the punishment for whatever the parent deemed they did wrong is that they cannot go to church. This is so egregiously wrong, just as wrong as it is for parents to put their children in the crosshairs of their own marital conflicts. Children must not be treated as pawns in the conflicts of a grown-up world.

Jesus sternly warned against all manner of withholding children from coming to Him.

> *13 Then people brought little children to Jesus for him to place his hands on them and pray for them. But the disciples rebuked them. 14 Jesus said, "Let the little children come to me, and do not hinder them, for the kingdom of heaven belongs to such as these." 15 When he had placed his hands on them, he went on from there.*
> *Matthew 19:13-15 NIV*

6 "If anyone causes one of these little ones—those who believe in me—to stumble, it would be better for them to have a large millstone hung around their neck and to be drowned in the depths of the sea. Matthew 18:6 NIV

5. At the close of the discipline, make sure to reaffirm the **value** of the child, as well as, reaffirming your love and God's love for that child. The parent who applied the discipline should also be the one to reaffirm their love for the child.

Parents and pastors have similar roles in bringing correction to those they have stewardship over in the Lord. Let us employ our responsibilities humbly as stewards of those He loves, always mindful of the grace and mercy we have also received from Him.

1 Brothers, if anyone is caught in any sin, you who are spiritual [that is, you who are responsive to the guidance of the Spirit] are to restore such a person in a spirit of gentleness [not with a sense of superiority or self-righteousness], keeping a watchful eye on yourself, so that you are not tempted as well. 2 Carry one another's burdens and in this way you will fulfill the requirements of the law of Christ [that is, the law of Christian love]. 3 For if anyone thinks he is something [special] when [in fact] he is nothing [special except in his own eyes], he deceives himself.[237]

• Helping the child to develop a deep love for Jesus Christ through their own personal loving relationship with Him.

Jesus Christ has always been my closest friend throughout life. As much as I dreaded disappointing my parents throughout my teenage

---

[237] Galatians 6:1-3 AMP

years, in like fashion, I did not want to disappoint Jesus. Of course, I was not/am not perfect, but even at a young age, I did know that what I wanted more than anything else in this life was to be in the center of God's Will and to be pleasing to Him.

As a teen, I used to ride my bike up and down the streets of our hometown all alone pouring my heart out in worship and prayer, "Jesus, whether You like it or not, You're stuck with me because I'm not leaving this relationship."

Crying my heart out to the Lord in this way helped to keep my heart close to Him and get me through my teenage years without caving to the temptations of the world around me.

If the sum total of a teenager's relationship with God only runs as deep as their church attendance, they will never survive the temptations and pressures around them. Jesus must be real to them. Of course, parents cannot force this to happen, but this is the goal for which we pray and live before them.

• Developing a lifestyle of daily devotions which include prayer, Bible reading and memorization.

As my brothers and I were growing into teenagers, our parents developed a practice of family reading time. We would take turns reading out loud with the rest of the family listening. We would do this regularly at home around the evening meal and also while traveling in the car during family vacations. Sometimes, we would read from the Bible and other times from a testimony or biographical book about the life of a missionary or minister. For example, one book I can recall reading together as a family was, *Like a Mighty Wind*, by Mel Tari, missionary to Indonesia. This family custom and the books we read had a profound impact on my life for Christ.

• Active and committed involvement in a Christ-centered, Word-based local church wherever availability allows. If children see both parents committed and serving in the local church, that example will more likely become their lifestyle too!

I often tell our church volunteers with school age children, "For the moment, your children are paying a price your involvement in serving God as they are with you at church extra days and hours when other kids are out playing. But as they grow older, they will begin to pay the price of their own service to God as they step into serving God at church for themselves."

Postmodern Christianity cannot accomplish these goals because it is too busy trying to impress and entertain kids rather than equip and arm them to be **insulated** in Christ. [238]

The Meteora monasteries can be seen from miles away. You look up and see them towering over you. It is super impressive! Those monasteries were built to **isolate** men and women away from the world around them, but in reality, they are a picture of how the disciple of Jesus Christ should be, standing out and shining before all as a city set on a hill in a spiritually dark world.

The challenge before the Church is to remain **insulated** from and uninfluenced by the customs, mindset, and values of the world without having to be **isolated** from it.

Colossians 2:6-7 offers clear counsel on how to do that,

> *6 Therefore as you have received Christ Jesus the Lord, walk in [union with] Him [reflecting His character in the things you do and say—living lives that lead others away from sin], 7 having been deeply rooted [in Him] and now being continually built up in Him and [becoming increasingly more] established in your faith, just as you were taught, and overflowing in it with gratitude.[239]*

---

[238] Romans 13:12; 2 Corinthians 6:7, Ephesians 6:10-17
[239] AMP Bible

To sum it up, these important lessons from church history teach us that:

True Biblical Christianity is not supposed to be a feel good, self-help entertainment system, but rather a life of shining propagation to the world and preparation to the believer for heaven.

CHAPTER SIXTEEN

GOD WORKS WITH REMNANTS

> *Yet I have reserved seven thousand in Israel, all whose knees have not bowed to Baal, and every mouth that has not kissed him.*
>
> *1 Kings 19:18*

Often times throughout church history, a particular stream or group will develop a very dogmatic theological position on something (beyond the core tenants of our faith). The position becomes so attached to and identified with the group who hold it so deeply that the group even forms new denomination or church organization as a result.

Sometimes, this process centers around a single word that becomes all-important to the doctrine. The word becomes so associated with that group's identity and doctrine that the rest of Christendom sheds use of it so as to not be mistakenly supporting a doctrinal position they may not believe in. This is unfortunate because otherwise perfectly good, neutral words become pariahs in the process as preachers and teachers stay away from them so as to not risk being misidentified as being associated with the group that has given the word such dogmatic meaning. It seems the word can no longer successfully be used in other contexts or to mean other things.

One example is the word rainbow. As Christians, we cherish the rainbow because of its role in the story of Noah and the covenant promise it gives us from God;[240] however, completely debase and immoral activist idealogues hijacked the rainbow and its colors and turned them into symbols for their perverse ideology and lifestyles. They have so ruined the beautiful, pure original meaning of the rainbow that it is often difficult for anyone else, especially Christians, to use it without people immediately mentally associating it with its meaning in the LGBTQwxyz movement first. A real tragedy.

As a side note, however, there are some positive developments as members of the LGBTQwxyz movement come to Christ and leave that lifestyle as this *Christianity Daily* article of June 12, 2021, reports, they are "taking back the rainbow," praise God!

> The 'rainbow revival' is a sign of God's covenant, says Angel Colon, who reportedly had 'miraculously survived' the Pulse Nightclub mass shooting in Orlando in June 2016. 'We are taking back the rainbow,' he said. 'It's His. For us, it's something beautiful.'
>
> 'We are here and we're loud, letting the world know that the rainbow is something beautiful,' Colon continued. 'And we shouldn't be ashamed of what it really is.'
>
> As the Freedom March activities continue, Colon and his friends are hearing from a growing number of individuals who want to abandon the LGBT lifestyle to follow Jesus.[241]

Jesus Christ is the only hope for *mankind!*

---

[240] Genesis 9:1-17

[241] christianitydaily.com/articles/12204/20210612/ex-lgbt-people-who-encountered-jesus-christ-are-taking-back-the-rainbow.htm

Let me give you another example of a similar nature.

Back in the early 1980s, the Catholic Church in the Philippines latched onto the word, "Charismatic," and started having Catholic Charismatic meetings as a new staple. They did this largely to stop the exodus of their members who were getting born-again and baptized in the Holy Spirit by being around Pentecostals. This was the way the Philippine Catholic Church kept these spiritually hungry members in the fold, by offering them "Charismatic" seminars and meetings. In just a short time, the word, charismatic, became so associated with the Catholic Church in the Philippines that true Charismatics could no longer use this word in the name of their church for fear of being misidentified as Catholics.

Of course, these so-called "Charismatic" meetings became so laced with deep Catholic doctrine that they hardly resemble any kind of genuine Charismatic Christianity at all. They operate more like a Catholic social club, devoid of true Holy Spirit power.

You just can't use the word, Charismatic, around a Filipino without them immediately thinking you are talking about something Catholic. Ironic, isn't it? To this day, whenever I use this word in speaking to a Filipino audience, I find myself clarifying all over again that I am not referring to anything Catholic but rather about people baptized in the Holy Spirit and operating in the Gifts of the Holy Spirit.

The word, remnant, is one of those perfectly good, neutral words which has been stigmatized in some parts of Christianity.

I once heard a preacher say that he would never use the word, remnant, except when the context was the "remnant nation of Israel." He had decided that it is not appropriate for Christians to use the word, remnant, in any other way or context.

The Seventh Day Adventist group has also taken this word hostage for one of their pet doctrines further stigmatizing it.

What a pity that this beautiful word has been stigmatized in some Christian circles because it is so linked to certain pet doctrines.

For clarification, I am not using the word in this chapter to push any pet doctrine. In my humble opinion, all that gets a little nutty and is totally unnecessarily. My use of the word here is not doctrinal but illustrational and very practical. I hope the reader will not read more into it than that.

Remnant comes from an old French word meaning, "remainder or remaining part." The Oxford English Dictionary defines remnant this way,

a part or quantity that is left after the greater part has been used, removed, or destroyed.

The believer must embrace the fact that for as long as we are living in this present life, those who truly belong to Christ will be in the minority. We must not harbor illusions of Christian majority in this life.

Christianity has never been the majority belief system in the world. Currently, it is estimated that there are about 2.3 billion Christians in a world population of eight billion. That figure would be much, much smaller if there was a way to count only those who are truly born-again. There are still so many souls needing harvesting for the Kingdom of God. The fields truly are white unto harvest.[242]

While Christianity is steadily growing in large parts of Asia, Africa, and South America in this 21st century, the numbers are in decline in the western cultures of Europe, Australia, and North America. Is Postmodern culture winning out in the West?

Have you ever felt like you were alone in serving God? Think again! God always has a people who are wholly and completely His. He has never been without a people He calls His own… and, He never will be.

In 1 Kings 19, Elijah thought he was the last faithful follower of God in the nation, but the Lord revealed to Elijah that He had 7,000 people

---

[242] John 4:35; Matthew 9:36-38

in Israel who still followed Him. Elijah was not alone, neither are you.

God has a solid record of working with remnants, and small amounts, small numbers, and small groups of people.
The Bible says in Zechariah 4:10,

10 Who dares despise the day of <u>small things</u>...[243]

Here are just a few examples from God's Word which affirm God's love for working with remnants, simple (humble) things, small amounts, small numbers, and small groups of people.

• Only eight people entered the ark saving the entire human race. Genesis 6:18; 1 Peter 3:20

• God preserved and then built the nation of Israel, first by sending Joseph ahead to Egypt alone, followed several years later by the whole clan of Israel numbering just seventy. Genesis 45:7; Genesis 50:20; Exodus 1:5; Deuteronomy 10:22

• God used the shepherd's staff Moses held in his hand to defeat Pharaoh and part the Red Sea. Exodus 4:2

• God opened the mouth of a donkey to warn the prophet. Numbers 22:21-39

• God sifted Gideon's army from 32,000 to 300 and then with just the 300 men of God's choosing, Israel defeated an enemy much larger and stronger. Judges Chapter 7

• David took just five smooth stones when fighting Goliath, but only needed one to kill him. 1 Samuel 17:40-50

• Elijah and the widow's container of flour and jar of oil used to sustain Elijah, the widow and her son in a time of famine. 1 Kings 17:14

• Elisha and the widow's jar of oil multiplied, saving her and her two sons from destruction. 2 Kings 4:1-7

---

[243] NIV (emphasis added)

- Elisha's twenty loaves of bread were multiplied and fed one hundred men. 2 Kings 4:42-44

- Jesus fed 5,000 men (plus women and children) with just five loaves of bread and two fish. Matthew 14:13-21

- Jesus fed 4,000 with seven loaves of bread and a few small fish. Matthew 15:32-39

- Jesus provides temple tax money for Himself and Peter through a coin in a fish's mouth. Matthew 17:24-27

- Jesus commended the widow's offering of just two mites in the temple as being of greater value than the donations of the wealthy. Luke 21:1-4

- Jesus used just twelve men to initiate the global propagation of His message and just 120 in the Upper Room on the Day of Pentecost to get His Church up and running. Luke 6:13; Matthew 10:1-4; Mark 3:14-19; Acts 1:12-15; 2:1-4

- God used Peter to heal the lame man at the gate called Beautiful with "only" the Name of Jesus. Acts 3:1-10

- The religious leaders in Jerusalem had no answer to the anointing upon Peter and John and the miracles they worked. They despised these men, yet marveled because they recognized that these men had "been with Jesus." Acts 4:13

- God needed "only" the unabashed praises of Paul and Silas in the Philippian jail to cause an earthquake that shook open the prison doors, setting Paul and Silas free, and resulting in the head jailor's whole household being saved! Acts 16:22-34

- God used the simple materials that Paul used in his trade as a tentmaker, his work aprons and sweaty face towels, to work miracles of healing to many. Acts 19:11-12

We could go on, but you get the idea, right?

Throughout church history there was always a remnant of believers who remained faithful to God. Even when the Roman religious machine was occupying Europe, remnants of true believers in Jesus Christ held fast throughout the years in the face of that powerful religious governmental system and in the midst of severe persecution as discussed in the foregoing chapter. Stories of the steadfast bravery of many of these remnant, minority believers are found in the famous book, *Foxe's Book of Martyrs*. Recommended reading by this author.

The rest of church history is replete with examples of God using small, humble things and people, small amounts/numbers, and remnants. God always has people who are exclusively His!

Never judge what God can do based on the size of the army He has to work with!

Don't limit God in your life just because you are not famous. Don't limit God in your church just because you may be few in numbers!

In 2000, the Lord began to impress upon me that our church here in Zürich, Switzerland, should own its own place rather than rent forever so I began to set that vision before our church leaders and very small congregation of many women and few men. We were about 60 in number when the Lord gave me this vision.

The whole story is too long to recount here but we began by setting up a building fund. The second step we took was to sow a very large amount of money into the building needs of a mission ministry in a developing nation. Finally, our church leaders began to search. We looked at every conceivable possibility: buying land and building from scratch, buying and renovating an existing building... We searched high and low for seven years. We took all these steps "by faith," not knowing at all how this vision could possibly come to fulfillment.

During that time, I would occasionally ask God, "Lord, why have You given this vision to our small, tiny, not-famous, insignificant church? We are like Gideon, the least of all churches in Zürich. Big, strong, famous churches can't afford to buy or build their own place. (Switzerland is such an expensive place and the culture, by and large, is to rent.) Why are You giving this vision to our very small church, Lord?"

Without missing a beat, the Lord would answer me every time I put that question to Him, "I'll do it just because you believe I can."

Nothing more. Nothing less. Nothing else.

Long story short, the Lord worked incredible financial miracles in our small, mostly women at that time, sixty or so strong member church and we moved into our own purchased facility in 2008, praise God!

Thirteen years later, God once again made the impossible possible as our small church of just around 120 was able to buy more space in our building, increasing our floor space by half.

Never discount what God can and will do with small things as Jesus declared in Mark 9:23 that all things are possible to the one who believes.

There is an old Pentecostal chorus that comes to mind when recalling the miracles that God has done. It goes like this:

God can do it again and again and again.[244]

He's the same God today as He always has been.

Yesterday and forever He's always the same.

There's no reason to doubt my God can do it again.

We serve the God of victory, healing, miracles, provision, and increase! Nothing is too difficult for our God![245]

Thank God for every big, famous, worldwide, mega ministry that is genuinely doing heaven's bidding. They have a reach that most of us will never have. However, I believe heaven will be filled much more with the testimonies of grandmothers who prayed their children and grandchildren into the Kingdom or into their ministry calling, and anonymous missionaries who lived out their lives diligently laboring for the Gospel in

---

[244] Composer unknown

[245] Jeremiah 32:17,27

foreign lands even though they never became famous nor had their stories told in bestselling books.

Heaven will be filled with the testimonies of small church pastors who faithfully and humbly shepherded their flocks through the storms of life, never abandoning nor abusing their position.

Heaven will be filled with the stories of people going to heaven because ordinary believers stood on street corners, day after day, handing out Gospel tracks.

Heaven will be filled with the testimonies of martyrs who remained faithful until death.

God invites us to be workers together with Him.[246] His only condition is that He is the boss, not you or me!

Just as He asked Moses, so will He ask you, "What is in your hand?"[247]

Offer it to God and watch Him use it! He can work with anything you have to offer Him. He can use the talent, gift, skill, or ability in your life if you will simply offer it up to Him.[248]

Moses offered God his shepherd's staff and God used Moses and his shepherd's staff to defeat Pharaoh, part the Red Sea, and lead a nation out of bondage. One man and his shepherd's staff.

Make yourself available to Him just as Saul (who later became the Apostle Paul) did the moment he came face to face with the Lord Jesus Christ in his road to Damascus conversion.

The first thing he did after confessing faith in Christ, was to ask this urgent question, "Lord, what do you want me to do?"[249]

Isaiah said to the Lord, "Here I am, Lord, send me."[250]

Why not tell the Lord, right now, that you are available for Him and then ask Him to show you what He wants you to do for His Kingdom and glory?

---

[246] 1 Corinthians 3:9; 2 Corinthians 6:1

[247] Exodus 4:2

[248] 2 Timothy 2:20-22

[249] Acts 22:10

[250] Isaiah 6:8

God does not place prerequisites of wealth, fame, beauty, or academic degrees on those He uses. I was a measly 19 years old when I got my start in missions and ministry. I had only a high school diploma and one year of liberal arts college on my side. I wrote to every missions organization operating around the world that I could find an address for asking them if I could become a missionary under their organization. Most never bothered to write back and the one or two organizations that did write back told me I was "too young and unqualified" to be a missionary. They told me to contact them after I got a Bachelor's, Master's, or PhD degree in nursing or Christian Ministry or Missiology, etc... Only then, would I be of use to them. But God had other plans for this very ordinary, nothing special Minnesota born and raised girl. Plans that *man's* organizations could not detect or recognize.

God loves to work with small (humble) things and people. He loves to demonstrate His power and glory in ways so that no flesh can take the credit.

He will always be in the midst of every remnant of believers who refuse to bow their knees to Baal (i.e.: the world and Postmodern philosophy and culture).[251]

We do not know what will come after Postmodernism should Jesus tarry, but if sociologists do identify and label an era after Postmodernism, you can be sure that the God who has worked with small things and remnants since the beginning of time, will still be working His miracles through them in the next era too should there be one, because He is...

Jesus Christ, the same yesterday, today and forever![252]

---

[251] 1 Kings 19:18

[252] Hebrews 13:8

CHAPTER SEVENTEEN

STAYING PURE IN AN IMPURE WORLD

> *To the pure, all things are pure; but to those who are defiled and unbelieving, nothing is pure, but both their mind and their conscience are defiled.*
> *Titus 1:15*

The phrase "staying pure" has gotten a bad rap in many Christian circles. It is often either mocked and made fun of as being outdated and old-fashioned or it is dismissed and ridiculed as coded language for Christian "legalism." The devil has done a real snow job on Postmodern Christians when it comes to the topic of Christian purity.

We have actually been making the same point over and over again in so many diverse ways to drive this central point home to the reader:

The life, values, and conduct of the believer, lover, disciple, and follower of Jesus Christ are to be vastly different from those of the world around them.

We are in trouble when we convince ourselves that "being like" makes us brighter lights and better Christians than "being unique" and set apart (from unsaved humanity) in thought, word, and deed.

Separated "from" and separated "unto"

In Romans 1:1, the Apostle Paul described himself in these three ways: (1) as a bond-servant of Christ Jesus, (2) called as an apostle, and (3) *set apart* for (or *separated unto*) the Gospel of God.

To be separated means to be sanctified and set apart for salvation and the grace of God.

Christian separation is a two-step system. Paul describes himself as separated *unto* the Gospel for God.

But we cannot successfully be separated *unto* something pleasing to God if we are not also separated *from* all that He hates.

Separation *from* is the first step to separation *to*. Too many Christians struggle in trying to separate from worldly things because they do not take the second step in moving closer to God (i.e.: separating *to*). Doing only the first half of the Biblical work of separation but skipping the *"unto"* part is sure way to end up with a Christian life which is heavy on rules and laws and light on grace and joy.

The notes on Romans 1:1 from the 1977 New American Standard Open Bible, page 1081, describe the importance of separation to the Christian life:

> **Without being separated, you can have relationship with God; but you cannot have fellowship with Him. You may be united to Him in Calvary, but separated from Him in sin (Isaiah 59:1,2 OT). Without separation, you can have influence without power, movement without achievement; you may try, but not trust; serve, but not succeed; war, but not win. Without separation _to_ God _from_ sin, your whole Christian life will be 'wood, hay, straw.' (Italics added)**

No wonder David cried out in Psalm 86:11,

...Give me an undivided heart that I may fear Your name.

That is what the believer needs, a heart that is completely and exclusively His.

Christian separation brings us to that place of intimacy and sweet fellowship with God like nothing else can.

"In" but not "of"

Jesus prayed for us in John 17. His prayer is known as the High Priestly Prayer. Among the things He prayed were these words:

14 I have given them Your word; and the world has hated them, because <u>they are not of the world</u>, even as I am not of the world. 15 I do not ask You to take them out of the world, but to keep them from the evil one. 16 <u>They are not of the world</u>, even as I am not of the world. 17 Sanctify them in the truth; Your word is truth. (emphasis added)

Earlier that same evening, He counseled His disciples to prepare themselves for the way forward, giving them the following instruction,

18 If the world hates you, you know that it has hated Me before it hated you. 19 If you were of the world, the world would love its own; but because <u>you are not of the world</u>, but I chose you out of the world, because of this the world hates you. 20 Remember the word that I said to you, 'A slave is not greater than his master.' If they persecuted Me, they will also persecute you; if they kept My word, they will keep yours also. John 15:18-20 (emphasis added)

1 Peter 2:9 and Titus 2:14 in the KJV describe the believer as being "peculiar." The intent of this word in the Greek is to describe God's people as being set apart from the world and to be exclusively His instead.

The 1978 edition of American Heritage Dictionary of the English Language includes the following definitions for the word *peculiar:*

1. Unusual, strange; 2. Standing apart from others, distinct and particular; 3. Exclusive, unique; 4. Belonging distinctly or especially to one person, group, or kind.

These definitions describe how the true disciple of Jesus Christ should feel in Modern and Postmodern culture.

In ways that count, we should feel just a little bit awkward, like we don't quite fit in, don't really belong here. It's not that we try to be odd in how we live but rather that the world will find our life (lifestyle, values, morals, and integrity) puzzling because it is so often unlike theirs.

If we want to stay pure in this Postmodern world, we must learn that it is okay to be "the odd man out" so-to-speak. For example, maybe everyone else in your workplace loves to go to your company's yearly Christmas party where a lot of drinking and debauchery goes on and they mock you for excusing yourself year after year. They are all trying to fit in and find acceptance, but you already know where you belong, so you go to your weekly Bible Study at church instead. Outwardly they mock you but, in their hearts, they actually respect you. The Bible says they do:

> *11 Beloved, I urge you as foreigners and strangers to abstain from fleshly lusts, which wage war against the soul. 12 Keep your behavior excellent among the Gentiles, so that in the thing in which they slander you as evildoers, they may because of your good deeds, as they observe them, glorify God on the day of visitation.*[253]

---

[253] 1 Peter 2:11-12

Years ago, I took a Christmas job at JC Penny, working there for about 3-4 weeks leading up to Christmas. My co-workers were friendly to me until, one-by-one, they asked me what I really do. As soon as I answered that I am a Christian missionary and minister, they all turned politely cold towards me and no longer invited me to sit with them during breaks. Their conversation was not for me anyway and I did not mind sitting alone. The Christian should not expect to be comfortable buddies with the world.

Settle it now once and for all in your heart, that you would rather be pleasing to God even if that means being misunderstood or rejected by unsaved people around you.[254]

Dirty Bible = Clean Life[255]

Seven-year-old Clarice[256] was learning to read, and her parents were doing a good job of teaching her and her older brother to read their Bibles regularly.

So, one day, she was reading to me from the Book of Psalms. When she finished, I took the opportunity to talk with her about how the believer should love God's Word and use their Bible like a workbook on how to live. I showed her my childhood Bible, another Bible of mine and my mom's Bible. All three well-worn Bibles had a lot of torn and taped together pages and were really marked up with highlights, underlines and notes scrawled about on most every page.

"Clarice," I said, "a dirty Bible very often means a clean life."

Clarice began to examine each Bible. She didn't understand that the "dirty" I talked about was all the underlining, highlighting and handwritten notes. When I realized that she thought I was talking about real dirt, with a smile in my heart, I began to explain to her that I was

---

[254] Matthew 10:34-40; Ephesians 5:7-10

[255] John 15:3; Ephesians 5:26-27

[256] An alias name used to protect the privacy of the real child.

talking about all the notes, underlining, and highlighting, etc. and she got the point.

Several weeks later, she picked up the Bible I currently use, opened it, and said, "Is this Bible dirty too?"

I replied, "Let's take a look inside."

As we looked at some of the "dirtier" pages, she exclaimed, "Wow! That's a lot of colors there!"

I pray that she will remember these moments and the lessons they bring as she grows up.

The Psalmist wrote,

> *9 How can a young man keep his way pure? By keeping it according to Your word.*[257]

Regardless of one's age, there's just no chance of *"keeping our way pure"* apart from reliance on the Word of God.

There is a saying, "Garbage in – Garbage out."

The Bible says,

> *15 To the pure, all things are pure; but to those who are defiled and unbelieving, nothing is pure, but both their mind and their conscience are defiled.*[258]

If we give ourselves to listening to and watching things filled with sexual themes, dirty jokes, crude talking, and violence, etc., we are going to end up taking on the spirit and mindset of whatever we feed ourselves. Guard your heart against offense![259]

Instead of Garbage in – Garbage out, let's cultivate our hearts and minds this way, "Purity in – Purity out."

---

[257] Psalm 119:9

[258] Titus 1:15

[259] Proverbs 4:20-27, especially verse 23

Fill your heart, mind, and mouth with these things mentioned in Philippians 4:8 (AMP Bible, emphasis added),

> *8 Finally, believers, whatever is true, whatever is honorable and worthy of respect, whatever is right and confirmed by God's word, whatever is __pure__ and wholesome, whatever is lovely and brings peace, whatever is admirable and of good repute; if there is any excellence, if there is anything worthy of praise, think continually on these things [center your mind on them, and implant them in your heart].*

Open your Bible in the middle and hold it out in your hand before you. With your free hand, trace around the edge of the book you are holding open. Then, say this to yourself,

"This is God's Word and edges of this book represent the borders for my life. I will live inside and keep myself inside the borders of God's Word."

Pursue Your God-given Purpose and Destiny

Remember the Biblical story of Esther? Her wonderful story of purpose and destiny is told in the Old Testament book named after her.

Esther had a choice to make. She could guarantee her life of luxury and comfort if she remained silent about the plans of Haman to exterminate the entire Jewish population in Persia.[260] Or, she could risk everything, including her very life, if she would attempt to intervene on behalf of the Persian Jews before the king. When she wavered, her uncle, Mordecai, reminded her that she had come to the position of queen for a purpose and that if she would falter in pursuing that purpose in its most important hour, she, too, would be swept away with the rest of her nation. Here are Mordecai's famous words in Esther chapter 4 (emphasis added),

---

[260] Esther chapter 3

13 Then Mordecai told them to reply to Esther, "Do not imagine that you in the king's palace can escape any more than all the other Jews. 14 For if you keep silent at this time, liberation and rescue will arise for the Jews from another place, and you and your father's house will perish. <u>And who knows whether you have not attained royalty for such a time as this?</u>"

Esther then understands that she was put on the earth for this momentous moment, so clothed with resolve cut from the cloth of destiny, Esther finds her courage in verse 16,

16 "Go, gather all the Jews who are found in Susa, and fast for me; do not eat or drink for three days, night or day. I and my attendants also will fast in the same way. And then I will go in to the king, which is not in accordance with the law; <u>and if I perish, I perish.</u>"

Her courage was rewarded with wisdom and success.

Nothing holds our feet to the fire like a sense of higher goal, calling, and purpose in life. The realization that God has specific plans and purpose for our lives helps to crystalize our focus. It becomes easier to let the passing pleasures and pains of this life fade by comparison, as we choose instead to pursue the destiny set out for us by the Lord of Heaven Himself! Keep your eyes on the big picture!

When I was young, I regularly cried out in prayer, "Lord, I want my life to count for Your Kingdom. Please, use me and make my life count, Lord."

If you pray that prayer in earnest God will answer you too, but it comes with a price. "Not my will, but Your Will be done, Lord,"[261] must be your prayer and your determination.

---

[261] Luke 22:42

Bucking Headwinds: Practice the "Not" Instead

Mark Twain once famously said,

Whenever you find yourself on the side of the majority, it is time to pause and reflect.[262]

As a rule of thumb, whatever is hip, chic, fashionable, "in," and popular in secular or church culture... practice the "not" instead. Whatever the crowd is going for, whatever the majority is doing, buying, craving, idolizing, and rallying around whether in material merchandise, activities, secular or church culture, train yourself to choose the "not" and practice the "not" instead.

For example, often times teenagers and young people in their early twenties claim that they want to be unique in their generation and then in complete irony, they fix their hair, body, and dress styles to perfectly mimic their contemporaries. There is nothing unique about that!

Walt Disney once said,

The more you are like yourself, the less you are like anyone else which makes you unique. The problem with most people is that they spend their lives trying to emulate others and so we have a lot of copies but few originals.[263]

I love to tell the young people in our church, "If you really want to have your own identity and be unique in your generation, then pretty much do the opposite of whatever your generation is doing. If the hairstyle for guys is long, keep yours short! If your school friends all go partying on the weekends, then you stay away from those parties. If your classmates are getting tattoos and body piercing, then you don't do those things so that you truly are unique in your generation. If your peers are addicted

---

[262] brainyquote.com/quotes/mark_twain_122378

[263] picturequotes.com/the-more-you-are-like-yourself-the-less-you-are-like-anyone-else-which-makes-you-unique-the-problem-quote-356667

to posting in social media apps, then be the one who steers clear of it. It's the only way you can truly be unique in your generation because if you do everything they are doing, you are not unique at all as you claim you want to be. You are a crowd follower instead of being someone who is thinking for themself as an individual."

When I was in high school, most of my classmates drank, smoked, or experimented with marijuana.

I can remember thinking to myself, "They are nice, funny and fun to be with when they are sober but act stupid when drunk."

They thought it was the other way around, but it wasn't.

Even in church culture, don't do things a certain way just because other ministers or churches are doing them. Just because something is the latest fad in church culture, etc. doesn't mean you have to copy it. Think and pray about the "why" of what you are doing, especially in church ministry. What is right for one church might not be the best for your church.

For example, about 25-30 years ago a fad got started in Philippine church culture where several of the teenage girls in the church dress up in long white dresses and dance, choreographed, at the front of the church with tambourines during the praise and worship. It is still the staple in most Filipino Full Gospel churches today. I've kept it out of our Bible School and campus church activities largely because I don't want our ministry to merely be a copy of whatever is the latest fad. I am determined that how we set church and ministry up at Rhema in the Philippines and AGAPE in Switzerland will be prayerfully decided based on God's Word and Will for these ministries, not on fleeting fashions and trends.

Practice the "not" instead.

Since the beginning of our church in 1995, our Sunday service time has been 2:00pm. Right in the middle of every Sunday afternoon! It came to be that way because the first rooms we rented were only available at that hour. Finally, towards the end of 1996, the Lord blessed us with a rented place of our own. Right away I inquired of the Lord as to what time we should change our service to. Should we change the time to 9am? 10am or 10:15? 10:30? How about 10:45? That is also a popular service time, after all, everybody knows that church meets on Sunday morning!

Try as hard as I could to convince the Lord, the only thing I heard in my spirit whenever I brought the subject up to the Lord was, "I never told you to change the time."

"Okay, Lord," I relented.

The ministry that He brought our church into over the years that followed proved God's wisdom right. We need an afternoon service because that is what works best for our church family and that's the way it has remained up to this very day.

Sometimes the right response is to do the complete opposite, but not always. It is probably safe to say that the right response to cultural fads and passing trends in any realm of life is somewhere between "doing the complete opposite" and "practicing the 'not' instead."

We can go to God for wisdom on the things we are unsure about… but most of the time, anything that is well loved by the world or well-loved by the masses even in Christendom, is enough of a clue to tell you to keep your distance from it.[264]

Too many Christians follow group think and mob mentality from both Christian and secular culture but as a disciple of Jesus Christ, our priority should always be to find out what God thinks about a matter or cultural practice or custom.[265]

When I went to Bible School, we were held to a strict dress code standard as students. We were taught to dress our best as representatives of Jesus Christ. That training of attention to personal excellence has stayed with me all these years.

---

[264] 1 John 2:15-17; 1 Peter 4:1-4

[265] Isaiah 2:22; John 12:43

The young men who serve in our church grew up with the habit of wearing suitcoat and tie to church on Sundays, not from a position of legalism, but because I taught our church that it is a good thing to look our best for the Lord and then set the example myself in how I am dressed for church.

So, when it started becoming fashionable for ministers and church workers to come to church dressed in raggedy clothes around 20-plus years ago, I just kept coming to church in skirt or dress. The ladies continued to come dressed up too because they did not see their pastor lower her dress standards. The men and young men who serve also continued to come in suit and tie because the men in our leadership came to church dressed that way.

I never made a law or rule about it, didn't have to. The leadership and I simply set the example which continues today. It is easy to see that people enjoy coming to church looking good for the Lord. Even school age kids come looking sharp! It is just part of our church culture now, but no worries, dear reader, for we do not make any attender who is not dressed up feel less important or less welcome.

How ironic, though, that the only people I have to inform to come dressed in suit and tie are guest speakers. When I have missed, they have come dressed in jeans and a casual shirt, so I don't miss anymore.

Bruce[266] was just a youngster and the drummer on our worship team back in the late '90s when it started becoming fashionable across most of the Church world to attend church (and preach) in ultra-casual clothing. He was so young that his drumbeat slowed down as the fast songs wore on because he would get tired!

I told him then, "Bruce, you might just as well keep your suitcoat and tie on because what goes around, comes around. Fads and fashions come and go. One day, someone will start what they believe to be a new trend

---

[266] An alias name used to protect the privacy of the real individual.

that makes dressing up for the Lord "in" again. When that happens, you will already be ahead of the curve. You will be in front of that fashion trend when everyone else thinks it is novel."

He is a husband and father now, serving in many areas of church ministry with his wife… and he is still wearing suit and tie to church on Sundays!

I've noticed that the cycle is slowing coming around full circle. Thirty-plus years ago, people came to church dressed up, both attenders and those on the platform. Twenty-five years ago, the trend began to shift dramatically to the point that wearing the super casual clothes was not only the style, but it was sold to the Church as the most anointed way to do church. But in the past five years or so, many ministers are beginning to dress a little better than they did 15-20 years ago…. What goes around, comes around. We might as well practice a Christianity that is not moved by culture but sets the example of stability for the sheep!

These stories about dressing up, etc. are just examples. They are **not** the main point. The main point is that, as believers, we need to be willing to practice the "not" instead, bucking the headwinds of culture, especially Postmodern culture!

Hanging in the youth room in our church is a poster of a comic-type underwater scene. Dozens of identical looking fish are swimming towards the bottom of the poster. One lone, brightly shining happy fish (looking something like Nemo) is swimming upstream against the flow.

The caption reads, "What is popular is not always right and what is right is not always popular."

It will be of increasing importance for us to be accustomed to practicing the not instead, the closer we get to the end of the age and the return of Christ.[267] If we want to remain pure in this generation, we must be willing to swim against the currents of popularity, especially those of modern-day culture.

---

[267] Luke 18:8; Hebrews 10:23-25

We must be willing to practice the "not" instead.

Don't Compartmentalize Your Faith

Many Christians make the mistake of compartmentalizing their life and morality from the Word of God.

Man has practiced compartmentalizing his moral conduct since the Fall of Adam but, once again, liberal theology, Modern, and Postmodern philosophy have mainstreamed it.

Do you know that you can take any verse of Scripture out of its setting and context and make it say anything you want? Doing that doesn't mean that the verse actually says what you want it to say or that the Word is really supporting your belief or conduct, etc. Doing that is a misuse and abuse of God's holy written Word.[268]

There are three big ways that we compartmentalize our faith:

First of all, when we pick and choose which verses to live by and ignore others, we are compartmentalizing our faith.

The Word of God, especially the New Testament, shows us what to believe and how to live. It is a self-defeating mistake to misuse God's Word by trying to bend it to justify or fit our beliefs, actions, and lifestyle, etc. Instead, it is our job to align our will and choices, conduct and character, beliefs, and lifestyle, etc. to the stable, constant, unchanging Word of Truth.

The Bible says,

> *15 <u>Study</u> to shew thyself approved unto God, a workman that needeth not to be ashamed, rightly dividing the <u>word</u> <u>of truth</u>.[269]*

---

[268] 2 Peter 1:19-20

[269] II Timothy 2:15 KJV, emphasis added

Other translations start this verse out with, "Work hard," "Do your best," "Make every effort," "Earnestly seek," and "Be diligent." If we are not diligent in our study of the Word of God, we are going to misuse it to justify a wrong belief or lifestyle we have. As followers of Jesus Christ, the first way we give evidence to our claim of faith is in our commitment and submission to the Word of God as the final authority over every area of our lives.[270]

If we want to stay pure in the midst of the ever-increasingly dark culture around us, we must be committed to the inerrant, supreme authority of God's Word.

Another way we might find ourselves compartmentalizing is when we hold to cultural customs which are clearly not supported in God's Word and rationalize doing so by reasoning, "Well, this is just our culture, e.g.: dishonesty, government corruption, drinking alcohol, worldly music, worldly dancing at weddings, etc." (Or whatever else one's cultural upbringing might be like.)[271]

So, in their minds, although they would not otherwise support these kinds of activities, they convince themselves that their engaging in these when culture calls for it does not actually conflict with or violate their Christianity in any way because they are operating in that moment in a different compartment of life. That is compartmentalizing.

Finally, we are compartmentalizing when we don't make the connection between our unChristlike conduct and our overall claim of faith.

Some Christians have really short fuses. They are moody and can explode on anyone around them without any self-awareness that they just sinned the sin of unbridled anger and unkindness.[272] Rather than

---

[270] Matthew 7:24-29; James 1:21-26

[271] Mark 7:1-13 (esp. 6-9,13)

[272] Proverbs 14:29, 15:18; Ecclesiastes 7:9; Ephesians 4:31; Colossians 3:8; James 1:19-20

issuing an apology for their hurtful conduct, they remain silent, or they try to justify their outburst with the commonly uttered justification for all ungodly behavior, "That is just the way I am." Filipinos say, "Ganyan lang talaga ako."

They are unable or unwilling to connect their outburst and bad character to Bible verses which condemn such behavior. To them, there is no inconsistency between the hurt and disrespect they hurl upon others and their overarching commitment to living the Christian life according to God's Word. This is a very ugly kind of believer compartmentalization.

No one who has been walking with the Lord for a few years should still be using the phrase, "That's just who I am," in defense of unChristlike character especially if they serve in church ministry, can quote all the verses in the Bible that warn against the unChristlike behavior, and can sit through every preaching and teaching nodding their heads in agreement with the Word being taught. At some point the believer must acknowledge and repent from the unChristlike character in their lives. To never make that connection and turn from both the behavior and the defense of it is to live in self-righteous hypocrisy.

Let the Word of God be the filter through which you see and process every detail and experience of life. Let your own personal life's "culture" be molded by nothing other than God's Word.

Stay Aglow in the Spirit
Romans 12:11 says,

> *11 Don't hesitate to be enthusiastic - <u>be on fire in the Spirit</u> as you serve the Lord!*[273]
> *11 never lagging behind in diligence; <u>aglow in the Spirit,</u> enthusiastically serving the Lord.*[274]

---

[273] CEB (emphasis added)
[274] AMP Bible (emphasis added)

One truly important component in helping us to stay pure in an impure world is the Baptism in the Holy Spirit. I would be remiss if I left it out for fear of alienating some readers.

Jesus is God's gift to the world. The Holy Spirit is God's gift to His Church. Salvation is God's gift to the world and the Baptism in the Holy Spirit is His gift to the Church. Hallelujah! Thank You, Lord, for the Holy Spirit!

The benefits and blessings of being filled with the Holy Spirit are innumerable.

If you are born-again, you have the Holy Spirit in you to bear witness with your spirit concerning your salvation, to help bring about the fruit of the spirit in you, and to help you grow in grace and Christlike character.[275] But when we are baptized in the Holy Spirit or filled with the Spirit, He comes upon our lives with His power to enable, empower, and anoint us for effective service for God.[276]

If you are already born-again, you can be filled with the Holy Spirit right now if you have not yet been clothed with power from on high. Just ask Jesus with childlike trust and faith to baptize you in the Holy Spirit. He will answer your faith and you will never be the same again.

I was baptized in the Holy Spirit at the age of 11 alone in my bed with the lights out one night before I was ready to go to sleep. I didn't even know what it was called. I did not know the theology of it nor the doctrine.

I just prayed a very simple, childlike prayer like this, "Jesus, whatever You did to Dad, do it me. Whatever You gave Dad, give it to me. I want it too."

I had heard my dad speaking in tongues and thought, "If it's good enough for Dad, then I want what he has from God."

---

[275] John 4:13-14; 7:37; 14:16-17; Romans 8:9; Galatians 5:22-23
[276] Matthew 3:11; John 7:38-39; Luke 24:49; Acts 1:4-5,8; 2:1-4; 8:14-17; 10:44-46; Acts 19:1-6

Well, I went to sleep that night filled with the Spirit and speaking in tongues.

Thank You, Lord, for the Holy Ghost.

He's my Comforter, my Helper.

On Him I do depend.

Thank You, Lord, for the Holy Ghost.[277]

I credit being baptized in the Holy Spirit as being a large part of how I made it through teenage years without surrendering to the temptations of the world. And, if not for the baptism in the Holy Spirit, I'm sure I would have quit the ministry or been defeated many times over these past 40 years!

God's Saving Power and Keeping Power

The salvation testimony of every believer falls into one of two categories of God's power: His saving power or His keeping power.

The "Saving Power" testimony is that of a person with a ruined past. A life full of sin, drugs, alcohol, criminality, immorality, rebellion, abortion, divorce, atheism, occultism, etc... until that person became born-again. This makes for a powerful, dramatic testimony of the saving power of God. It is exciting to listen to.

The "Keeping Power" testimony is far less dramatic! Some might even describe it as boring! It is the testimony of the keeping power of God at work in someone who comes to faith in Christ at an early age and simply never does fall into false belief systems, sinful vices, or immoral living. It is the keeping power of God which brings that young person through their youth and keeps them from the major vices of sin.

Years ago, I put forth a challenge to the 10-12 year-olds in our church during a Sunday service. I offered 500 Swiss Francs (about US$500 of

---

[277] © Words and Music by Keith Moore

my own personal money, not church money) to any 10-12 year-old who would enter into and successfully complete a "covenant" with me. The covenant stated that the child promised to never try, even once, a taste of any alcohol. Not one puff of a cigarette was allowed. They promised never to try any kind of drugs, not even one try, or to go to bars and nightclubs or to do worldly dancing, get body piercing or tattoos, or engage in any kind of premarital sexual act, etc. They promised to stay close to Jesus by staying close to church. All this they promised until the age of 23. And, if they messed up, even once, the covenant was broken and made void.

If they succeeded, I would give them the 500 Swiss Francs they had earned in a church service. They were responsible up to their 23rd birthday. My goal was to challenge the child to get to 23 years old without falling into any of those worldly vices. I figured if they could do that, then the probability would be very high that they would continue to live that way for the rest of their lives. They had to sign the covenant paper I drew up, a parent signed, and I signed.

Seven children accepted my challenge and offer that day. I began to worry about how I was going to save up a potential CHF3,500 should they all succeed over the next 11-13 years! Somehow, I knew that it was very unlikely that all seven would make it. I did desire for them all to make it even though that result would cost me CHF3,500 (US$3,500).

Only one young man named, Mac,[278] succeeded. I knew from the start that if any of them did make it, it would be Mac because he had a relationship with Christ that far surpassed the others.

He had kept that covenant from the age of 11 and throughout his teenage years. Twelve years in total.

I kept my part of the covenant by presenting CHF500 in cash to him during one Sunday service near to his 23rd birthday. I had confidence in his integrity and honesty, that he did, in fact, keep

---

[278] An alias name used to protect the privacy of the real individual.

the covenant. He is still faithfully serving in our church today and he is a part of the next generation of leaders that I hope to hand the church over to one day in the future.

What a wonderful modern day testimony of God's keeping power in this young man's life. To God be the glory! I encourage Christian parents, grandparents, godparents, uncles, and aunts to pray about making a similar type of covenant pact with a 10-12 year old in your life. Perhaps, it will provide the help, inspiration, and motivation that child needs to get through their teen years without falling to all kinds of sinful choices.

If the Church is not careful, it will end up over-glamorizing the Saving Power testimonies while inadvertently, and perhaps unintentionally, shunning the Keeping Power testimonies as giving off a "too-holier-than-thou" impression.

A Swiss father once told me when his teenage son was caught smoking, that it is "just normal, just a part of growing up" for kids to experiment with things like drinking, smoking, drugs, sex, etc. before they can really decide whether or not they want those things in their lives. Aye-yai-yai!

I immediately replied, "No, it is not normal. It's not necessary that a teenager try sin in order to find out they don't want the consequences of that vice in their life.

"First of all, one try is all it takes for some kids (and grown-ups too) to become addicted to a substance for life. And, secondly, kids need to know that they do not have to try or experience sin in order to find out they do not want the consequences from sin in their lives, just like you and I don't have to rob a bank in order for us to find out or realize that we don't like being in jail!"

Praise God for both kinds of testimonies, but I pray that every Christian parent and every pastor will strive to guide children that it is far better to grow up and live in God's keeping power rather than to run wild as a prodigal son or daughter and then need His saving power.

There is a wise proverb that says, "it is easier to grow a straight tree (by guiding its shape straight from the start), than to straighten out a full-grown tree which is already crooked."

Parents and pastors, be proactive in putting forward adults, both young and old, with "Keeping Power" testimonies, like Mac, as role models and heroes for your younger children to follow.[279]

Deep or Wide?

One of the graduates from our Bible School in the Philippines is the busiest non-famous man I have ever met. I'll call him Peter here although that is not his real name.

Peter pioneered a church many years ago. He does all the usual church ministry: pastor, preach, train his leaders and young people, etc. But on top of all that, he coaches a local community basketball team, he teaches some classes in a high school and a few in college, and he is taking more higher education classes in order to secure a full-time teaching position in a local university. He still squeezed in time to teach a course or two in our Bible School which required him to travel two hours one way to get to our Bible School. And, in addition to all that, he is a widower and father of three children of high school and college age. He is constantly on the go every single day.

One day, I said to him, "Peter, you are the busiest man I have ever met," and then I began to explain to him the two ways that each of us invest our lives: widely or deeply.

To invest yourself "widely" means that you are busy with many projects and invitations beyond the scope of your pastoral work, hence the phrase, "spreading ourselves too thin." Some head pastors are away from their congregations far more than they are home with the sheep.

---

[279] 1 Corinthians 4:16; 1 Corinthians 11:1; Philippians 3:17

If this is really God's Calling upon your life then it might be worth a second prayer to find out from the Lord if you are really where you need to be in pastoring. Maybe some kind of traveling ministry better suits your gifts, desires, and leanings?

Pastor, to invest your life "deeply" means that you are, for the most part, a stay home pastor who is focused on the relationship you have with the sheep God entrusted to your care. You share in the daily lives, victories and struggles of the sheep. You know the sheep and they know you. You go through life together: laugh together, cry together, rejoice together, etc. You don't outsource your pastoral responsibilities to YouTube. You know God put you in the midst of that sheepfold to lay down your life as you take care of theirs with His help. The joy you experience comes from watching the sheep grow, much like how parents take joy in watching their children grow.

1 Peter 5:1-4 gives this command coupled with a promise,

> *2 take care of the group of people you are responsible for. They are God's flock. Watch over that flock because you want to, not because you are forced to do it. That is how God wants it. Do it because you are happy to serve, not because you want money. 3 Don't be like a ruler over those you are responsible for. But be good examples to them. 4 Then when Christ the Ruling Shepherd comes, you will get a crown—one that will be glorious and never lose its beauty. (ERV Bible)*

As pastors, of course we want to reach the world with the Gospel but let's remember to be faithful and focused on the needs of the sheep God has already entrusted to us, even if they number only twenty![280] Let their spiritual wellbeing be our priority over any desire to get thousands of

---

[280] Luke 16:10; Revelation 2:10

followers, views or likes from complete strangers in social media. May we have ears to clearly hear the counsel of the Good Shepherd for our churches,[281] holding onto the same with the determination of a bulldog on a bone and letting every other ambition fade by comparison.

I don't believe that any person, except Jesus, can successfully invest their life both widely and deeply with equal zeal and energy and still be truly fruitful.

Why do we do it?

Why do we do it? Why do believers strive to live free from the sinful pleasures this world offers? Why are we willing to forego unbiblical cultural norms since we are under grace and not under Old Testament Mosaic Law? Why are we willing to be the odd-man-out in thought, word, and deed, in the midst of our generation and peers? Why would we give willful effort to stay pure in an impure world? Why do it?

Perhaps this will surprise you, but the answer probably has less to do directly with salvation and going to heaven than you might think, for the Bible makes it clear that we are not saved on the basis of good works or good behavior and conduct but by the unearned, undeserved grace of God.[282] We cannot earn our way into heaven, nor does God expect us to pay for our salvation through some kind of post-salvation good behavior installment plan.

Here are four simple yet profound reasons that answer the question why:

1. It is our desire to be pleasing to the One who saved us, the Lover of our soul.

Even if we could name no other reason, this should be more than enough reason and motivation to live our lives circumspectly.

---

[281] John 10:1-16

[282] Ephesians 2:8-9; Titus 3:5

These verses remind us that we are to live every day,

10 trying to learn what is pleasing to the Lord.[283]

And again,

9 Therefore we make it our aim, whether present or absent, to be well pleasing to Him.[284]

The price of Christ's redemptive work for our salvation, described in 1 Peter 1:14-19, is too precious to be treated carelessly,

14 As obedient children, do not be conformed to the former lusts which were yours in your ignorance, 15 but like the Holy One who called you, be holy yourselves also in all your behavior; 16 because it is written: "You shall be holy, for I am holy." 17 If you address as Father the One who impartially judges according to each one's work, conduct yourselves in fear during the time of your stay on earth; 18 knowing that you were not redeemed with perishable things like silver or gold from your futile way of life inherited from your forefathers, 19 but with precious blood, as of a lamb unblemished and spotless, the blood of Christ.

2. It is His nature at work in us.

The Bible says,

Therefore if any man be in Christ, he is a new creature: old things are passed away; behold, all things are become new.[285]

---

[283] Ephesians 5:10

[284] 2 Corinthians 5:9 NKJV

[285] 2 Corinthians 5:17

The believer who is comfortable in worldly environments and conversation just isn't living after the new nature. We can't always avoid every worldly moment or situation, but we shouldn't be enjoying them.[286]

Let's live after the new creation nature of Christ in us.

3. Our testimony to the world around us requires it.

I do believe that we have not failed to make this point over and over again throughout this book.

There is a famous saying that reminds us that our lives are the only Bible that some unbelievers will ever read… What are they reading in the Bible of your life, conversation, character and values? The world around you is watching how you live. What do they see?

4. Our belief that there is greater reward awaiting us for remaining faithful to God. Reward that comes in God's timing in this life and the promise of reward for faithfulness in the life to come.

Christians believe in heaven. We believe in eternal life and eternal reward. We believe in the principle of delayed reward or delayed/ deferred gratification. We are willing to live a self-disciplined life now because we believe God's promises regarding reward in this life and in eternity.[287]

Consider these verses:[288]

> *7 But you, be strong and do not lose courage, for there is reward for your work. 2 Chronicles 15:7*

> *21 His lord said to him, 'Well done, good and faithful servant; you were faithful over a few things, I will make you ruler over many things. Enter into the joy of your lord.' Matthew 25:21*

---

[286] Romans 6:11-18; Ephesians 4:22-24; Colossians 3:5-10; Hebrews 10:26

[287] Hebrews 11:24-26; 1 Corinthians 3:14

[288] All taken from the NIV translation unless otherwise noted.

29 "Truly I tell you," Jesus said to them, "no one who has left home or wife or brothers or sisters or parents or children for the sake of the kingdom of God 30 will fail to receive many times as much in this age, and in the age to come eternal life." Luke 18:29-30

6 Therefore humble yourselves under the mighty hand of God, so that He may exalt you at the proper time. I Peter 5:6 (NASB)

9 And let us not grow weary while doing good, for in due season we shall reap if we do not lose heart. Galatians 6:9

14 If what has been built survives, the builder will receive a reward. 1 Corinthians 3:14

10 For we must all appear before the judgment seat of Christ, so that each of us may receive what is due us for the things done while in the body, whether good or bad. 2 Corinthians 5:10

17 For our light affliction, which is but for a moment, is working for us a far more exceeding and eternal weight of glory. 2 Corinthians 4:17

25 And everyone who competes for the prize is temperate in all things. Now they do it to obtain a perishable crown, but we for an imperishable crown. 1 Corinthians 9:25

58 Therefore, my beloved brethren, be steadfast, immovable, always abounding in the work of the Lord, knowing that your labor is not in vain in the Lord. 1 Corinthians 15:58

7 I have fought the good fight, I have finished the race, I have kept the faith. 8 Finally, there is laid up for me the crown of righteousness, which the Lord, the righteous Judge, will give to me on that Day, and not to me only but also to all who have loved His appearing. 2 Timothy 4:7-8

12 And behold, I am coming quickly, and My reward is with Me, to give to every one according to his work. Revelation 22:12

The Bible lists at least five crowns in the New Testament which are prepared for distribution at the Judgment Seat of Christ.[289] These crowns are not given out automatically to all believers. Rather, Jesus will award them to those who "earned" them in this life as a result of accomplishing the criteria associated with each.[290]

It is within the bounds of righteousness for us to desire to "earn" crowns in this life and to not enter heaven empty-handed.

Revelation 4:10 explains what we will be doing with the rewards and crowns we receive from the Lord for doing His Will in this life. We will not be gloating with pride over any acclaim we received during this life nor as the result of our life and works on earth. Instead, we will turn those very rewards and crowns into objects of worship as we cast them at the feet of Jesus.

Heaven is the place of ultimate purity. Let us ready our lives for it by developing purity here and now in character, thought, word, and deed so that we will not feel out-of-place when we get to that place of ultimate purity and rapturous splendor!

---

[289] 1 Corinthian 9:24-27; Revelation 2:10; 1 Thessalonians 2:19-20; Philippians 4:1;

[290] 2 Timothy 4:5-8; 1 Peter 5:4; 2 Corinthians 5:10

2 Corinthians 5:9-10

CHAPTER EIGHTEEN - EPILOGUE

COMING OUT ALIVE!

"

Be faithful until death,
and I will give you the crown of life.
Revelation 2:10

So much has changed just since I began writing this book in 2017. From the end of 2016 until the COVID-19 pandemic slammed into the world in early 2020, life in America was sailing along and the whole world benefitted from America's stability, peace and prosperity during these few short years. But now, with the residual effects of the COVID-19 pandemic lingering on, another page for humanity has turned once again and we are living witnesses to the unfolding turbulent political, cultural, and spiritual events around us.

This is the second watershed event for the world in the short span of just twenty years (since 9-11). It is very unusual for the world to experience two world-order-altering events in such a short span of time. I believe we can conclude from this that the ticking of the clock of humanity is speeding up (or winding down, whichever way you choose to look at it). It would be difficult for the Bible-believing Christian to conclude otherwise.

Some of the material included in chapter six in particular, may prove to already be outdated by the time this book is released largely because life and church practices have been changing of necessity as a result of government-led pandemic restrictions and lockdowns. Changes which only further prove the point as to just how quickly the world and Church, trends, fads and fashions change. However, I am leaving that material in the book to make the point that much of the Postmodern Church has been so busy enjoying the "fat" years from the early 1990s up to 2020, that it has almost missed completely on truly preparing the Body of Christ for the "lean" years which could be coming upon us (i.e.: harder times for believers and churches). [291]

Because of the relative level of peace in the world for the past 25-30 years, the sleeping Postmodern Church has been preoccupied, filling its belly with the fat of high-powered, entertainment-based, star-chasing, culture-appeasing, fads-focused Christianity.[292]

Did the Postmodern Church so convince itself over the past quarter of a century that there would be no harm or danger, no consequence in welcoming so many worldly and cultural values, fads, fashions, and priorities into its house?[293]

Now, it seems the world is entering what looks to be some of the most spiritually violent years since Christ walked the earth. We

---

[291] Genesis chapter 41

[292] Ephesians 5:13-18

[293] 1 Peter 4:17 (None of the views in this book are intended to come across as critical, judgmental, sarcastic or cynical. Each observation made and every question asked are made and asked with sobering sincerity.)

are quite possibly standing at the front door of the fulfillment of all remaining Biblical end time prophecies.

Church can't be about "cool" and entertainment and warm cultural fuzzies anymore. The true Church of Jesus Christ must prepare to face increasing opposition, discrimination, persecution, and rejection in the years to come. To believe less is to stick one's head in the sand… to use the analogy of the ostrich.

For many in certain streams of Christianity, talk of difficulty or persecution for the Western Church is considered defeatist and lacking in faith. Sadly, the Western Church has been fed the line for several decades that it will be spared from all forms of rejection, persecution, discomfort, and suffering… that such hardships were only meant for Christians throughout church history and for people in faraway lands but not for Western Christianity. Daily, however, the news testifies that the reality is turning out differently. Incidences of hatred, discrimination and persecution against Christians and churches from both society and government are on the rise in historically safe countries such as the U.S., Canada, and the U.K. at an alarming rate.

It is time for the Church to refocus on preparing believers to be strong in the Lord, well-trained in His Word, and faithful in the face of increasing opposition, for this, too, is the message of victory and overcoming faith.

I encourage the reader to search for a home church which is faithfully delivering the uncompromised, unadulterated Word of God if you can. One that challenges you to live a pure and godly life, and humbly endeavors to live that dedicated life themselves. If you find one like that, get in and be faithful and supportive of it because there are literally millions of hungry believers all over the world who dream of having such a church family around them. Learn to not sweat the small stuff, i.e.: minor insults, rubbings, corrections, and offenses.

Let's say, for example, that Margaret brings flowers to church which she intended for use at the front of the sanctuary near the pulpit on the following

Sunday, but instead, the person responsible for all flower arrangements in the church put them on display in the foyer. Sadly, that would be enough for some "Margarets" to justify leaving the church stinging from the insult.

Ask yourself this question when you face such moments, "Is this situation and the energy and emotion I am investing in it right now so all-fired important that it will even matter in five years or 10 or in eternity?"

If the answer comes back, "No," then ask the Lord to help you train yourself to forgive quickly, let go, and forbear in the disappointments of life and the small interpersonal relationship rubbings of life which are inconsequential in eternity… especially in your family and in the local church. In other words, don't sweat the small stuff! Bro. (Kenneth E.) Hagin used to say, "Be quick to repent. Quick to forgive. And, quick to believe."

If you are reading this book in an area of the world where you have no access to a church, do not be discouraged. God will strengthen and carry you where you are. He knows your heart and sees your needs. It is my prayer that the information contained herein will aid in equipping you to overcome in life as you pass through this Postmodern world.

I will finish where I began, with the promises made by the Lord Jesus to the seven churches in the Book of Revelation.

> *2:7 "He who has an ear, let him hear what the Spirit says to the churches. To him who <u>overcomes</u> I will give to eat from the tree of life, which is in the midst of the Paradise of God."*

> *2:11 "He who has an ear, let him hear what the Spirit says to the churches. He who <u>overcomes</u> shall not be hurt by the second death."*

> *2:17 "He who has an ear, let him hear what the Spirit says to the churches. To him who <u>overcomes</u> I will give some of the hidden manna to eat. And I will give him a white stone, and*

on the stone a new name written which no one knows except him who receives it."

2:26 "And he who <u>overcomes</u>, and keeps My works until the end, to him I will give power over the nations— 27 'He shall rule them with a rod of iron; They shall be dashed to pieces like the potter's vessels'— as I also have received from My Father; 28 and I will give him the morning star. 29 "He who has an ear, let him hear what the Spirit says to the churches."

3:5 "He who <u>overcomes</u> shall be clothed in white garments, and I will not blot out his name from the Book of Life; but I will confess his name before My Father and before His angels. 6 He who has an ear, let him hear what the Spirit says to the churches."

3:12 "He who <u>overcomes</u>, I will make him a pillar in the temple of My God, and he shall go out no more. I will write on him the name of My God and the name of the city of My God, the New Jerusalem, which comes down out of heaven from My God. And I will write on him My new name. 13 He who has an ear, let him hear what the Spirit says to the churches."

3:21 "To him who <u>overcomes</u> I will grant to sit with Me on My throne, as I also <u>overcame</u> and sat down with My Father on His throne. 22 He who has an ear, let him hear what the Spirit says to the churches."

Each promise made in these verses is predicated on the believer overcoming something in this life.

The word, overcome(s), in the Greek is, *nikao*, meaning,

> **to conquer; to carry off the victory, to come off victorious - of Christians that hold fast their faith even unto death against the power of their foes, and temptations and persecutions.**[294]

Jesus told us ahead of time that we would face trouble in this world when He said in John 16:33,

> *33 I have told you these things, so that in Me you may have [perfect] peace and confidence. In the world you have tribulation and trials and distress and frustration; but be of good cheer [take courage; be confident, certain, undaunted]! For I have overcome the world. [I have deprived it of power to harm you and have conquered it for you.] (AMPC)*

What a promise! Not a promise that we will never experience rejection or persecution in this life. Jesus forewarned us in this verse that we will indeed face troubles of every kind. In 1 Peter 4:12, Peter reiterated the warning that we should not be surprised when facing opposition to our faith, persecution, and tribulation.[295]

The promise Jesus made in the verse above is that in Him and by Him and through Him we overcome every hardship. There is no shortage of verses in the Bible assuring the believer in Christ of ultimate victory over every tribulation of this life.

The Apostle Paul wrote that we are overcomers, more than conquerors, and that through Christ, we always triumph.[296]

It is the Will of God for every child of His to come out on the other side of this Postmodern Era (spiritually) alive and well in the Lord! With

---

[294] biblestudytools.com/lexicons/greek/nas/nikao

[295] 1 Peter 4:12

[296] Romans 5:3-5; 8:37; 1 Corinthians 15:57; 2 Corinthians 2:14

oil in our lamps,[297] strong in the Lord,[298] victorious, and unstained in our character, thoughts, words, and deeds by the filth of this world and its culture.[299]

Christian believer in Jesus Christ, you and I do not have to be swallowed up by Postmodern philosophy and culture! We cannot avoid the fact that we are living in this Postmodern time and culture, but it is imperative that we remain unstained by it. Rise above it, dear saint! Begin now to live your life independent of every influence that comes from this world and its mindset.

We are not poor, helpless victims in this Postmodern war nor in the battles that await us in any possible future epoch yet unnamed. We are sons and daughters of the King of kings and the Lord of lords!

In Luke 18, Jesus forewarned us that constant prayer and persistent faith in God which remains undeterred, by either opposition to our faith on the left hand or the comfort of familiar culture on the right, would be essential to the believer's fortitude as we approach the end of the age.

> *1 Now Jesus was telling the disciples a parable to make the point that <u>at all times they ought to pray and not give up and lose heart,</u>*
>
> *8 I tell you that He will defend and avenge them quickly. <u>However, when the Son of Man comes, will He find [this kind of persistent] faith on the earth?</u>*[300]

Yes, we find challenges to the left and challenges on the right in life, but they are no match for the promises and power to overcome that we have in our great God! We will keep our eyes fixed and focused on Christ

---

[297] Matthew 25:1-13

[298] Ephesians 6:10-17; 1 Corinthians 15:54-58; 16:13-14; 2 Corinthians 12:9-10

[299] James 1:27; Psalm 19:14

[300] Luke 18:1-8 AMP Bible (emphasis added)

Jesus our Lord, the Author and Finisher of our faith[301] for He is faithful to deliver us out of them all![302]

In order for us to "come out alive," we must let the Word of God form our culture instead of the dictates of society around us. We must focus more on the "heavenly dream" than the "American dream" or any other ambition which follows after this world's value system. Use everything in your life, every educational attainment, every skill and talent, as a tool in representing the heart of God, advancing His Kingdom in your sphere of influence.[303]

Let us love His appearing (both His advent 2,000 years ago and His second coming) more than we love our houses, cars and bank accounts… more than we love life itself. Maranatha![304]

May our all-consuming passion be to:

Go where He wants us to go.

Say what He wants us to say.

Think what He wants us to think.

Love what He wants us to love.

'Hate' what He wants us to hate.

Do what He wants us to do.

And be who He wants us to be.

Nothing more. Nothing less. Nothing else.

2 Timothy 4:8 says that the crown of righteousness will be waiting for us if we love His appearing above all else, loving not our lives (giving our own pleasures priority over doing His Will and pleasure) even unto death.[305]

---

[301] Proverbs 4:25-27; Hebrews 12:2

[302] Psalm 34:6-7, 17,19; 37:23-24; 2 Timothy 3:11

[303] 1 Peter 4:10-11

[304] 1 Corinthians 16:22

[305] Revelation 2:10; 12:11

Music has always been a very important part of my walk with Jesus, so I leave you with the lyrics of one of my favorite hymns, *Blessed Assurance*, by Fanny Crosby. [306]

Blessed assurance, Jesus is mine;
Oh, what a foretaste of glory divine!
Heir of salvation, purchase of God,
Born of His Spirit, washed in His blood.

This is my story, this is my song,
Praising my Savior all the day long.
This is my story, this is my song,
Praising my Savior all the day long.

Perfect submission, perfect delight,
Visions of rapture now burst on my sight;
Angels descending, bring from above
Echoes of mercy, whispers of love.

Perfect submission, all is at rest,
I in my Savior am happy and blest;
Watching and waiting, looking above,
Filled with His goodness, lost in His love.

God has called us. In Christ, He has equipped us to COME OUT on the other side of Postmodernism ALIVE and well, without spot or wrinkle![307]

His Church is indeed COMING OUT ALIVE!

Be part of it.

---

[306] ©1873 Words by Fanny Crosby (1820-1915), Music by Phoebe P. Knapp (1839-1908)
[307] Ephesians 5:26-27

WHERE WOULD YOU BE WITHOUT JESUS?

The Lord gave me this song a few years ago. May the message in these lyrics speak to your heart. It's called, *Believing*.[308]

What is real?

Is it only what you feel?

Can't believe?

Not unless you see it for yourself?

To see is to believe, they say.

Still you hope there is another way.

Faith is such a mystery,

Believin' in your heart's the key, the way.

There is a Redeemer,

Who laid down His life.

He calls us to follow,

By faith and not by sight.

Blessed is the man who puts his trust in Him.

Who though he has not seen, still believes.

So give up every doubt today,

Cause Jesus is the only Way.

Who could ever love you more,

Than He who is the Open Door to life?

[308] ©2007 Words & Music by Karen Cedergren

You <u>can</u> go to heaven without...

Fathers, Mothers, Husbands, Wives,
Children, Family, Friends, Religion,
Education, Money, Titles, Honors,
Awards, Fame, Fortune, Achievements,
Positions, Possessions, Lands, Houses,
Gold, Jewelry, Cars, Computers,
Cell phones, Technology, Internet,
and everything else that belongs to this life,

But you <u>cannot</u> go to heaven without... JESUS !!!

Dear Friend,

Jesus loves you! The Bible says in John 3:16,

> ***"For God so loved the world (you), that He gave His only begotten Son (Jesus), that whosoever believes in Him should not perish, but have everlasting life!"***

and again,

> ***"... God has given us eternal life, and this life is in His Son (Jesus). He who has the Son has the life..." (I John 5:11,12)***

You can know with assurance that heaven is your home!

Pray this prayer with all your heart and simple childlike faith, and receive eternal life today in Jesus' name:

"Lord Jesus, I confess to You that I am a sinner and cannot save myself. I believe that You died on the cross to pay for my sins and rose from the dead to give me everlasting life. Come into my heart and make me a new person on the inside. I give my life to You and I confess You now as the Lord and Saviour of my life.

Fill me with Your Holy Spirit and help me to live for You and serve

You forever. Thank You for making me a child of God in Your Name, Amen."

********* ********* ********* ********* ********

Once you have accepted Christ, take these important steps to begin to GROW as a Christian:

1. Talk with God every day from your heart in prayer. (John 16:23-27; Philippians 4:6)

2. Tell another believer that you have accepted Jesus into your heart and have become a Christian. (Matthew 10:32-33)

3. Read the Bible daily, beginning with the Gospel of John. (Psalms 119:105)

4. Attend a Bible-believing church where the Lordship of Jesus Christ is believed and preached; where you can hear the full counsel of God's Word and have fellowship with other believers. (Hebrews 10:22-25; I Peter 2:2)

ABOUT THE AUTHOR

Karen was born and raised in Minnesota, USA, but has known the Call of God in her life for Christian missions since the age of four. She has more than 40 years of missions and full-time Christian ministry experience, having lived most of her life outside the U.S. (in Africa, Asia, and Europe). Karen graduated from RHEMA Bible Training Center (College) in 1983. She is Cofounder (1983) and President of Rhema Christian Center Philippines Inc. which includes a Bible School for adults, church and preschool. In 1995, she planted a multi-national, English-speaking church in Zürich, Switzerland, where she continues to live and pastor. Ordained into the ministry at the age of 23 by her U.S. covering organization, Rhema Christian Center, Karen is also one of the earliest members of RHEMA Ministerial Association International (RMAI), Tulsa, OK. She has written dozens of worship songs and her passion is teaching God's Word using everyday illustrations that make the Word easy to understand. Karen's rich, forty-plus years of missional lifestyle and church ministry experience qualify her to dive into the subject matter of this book from a unique perspective.

ACKNOWLEDGMENTS

Heartfelt thanks and appreciation to the following people for their help to me with this book:

To my proofreaders, Tess Solis and Sue Ehn.

To Rev. Ed Garcia, Rev. Peter Barfoot, and Rev. John Grunewald for taking time to read my manuscript in its prepublication form.

To Chloe, my photographer.

To Setsuri Solis, for her wonderful art, graphics, ad work, and cover design concept. Copyright is claimed on all her work. All rights reserved.

GLOSSARY OF TERMS

Greatest Generation (Elders) – (Born 1901 – 1927)

The Silent Generation – (Born 1928 – 1945)

Baby Boomers – (Born 1946 – 1964)

Generation X (Gen X-ers) – (Born 1965 – 1983)

Millennials (and Gen Y) – (Born 1984 – 1998)

Generation Z (Gen Z-ers) – (Born 1999 – 2012)

Generation Alpha (Gen Alpha) – (Born 2013 – mid 2025) This group is aptly called "Gen Alpha" because they are the first generational group entirely born in the 21st century.

Cancel Culture – "[Cancel culture] means rewriting history and stopping the acknowledgment of facts because they are offensive to a racial, religious, ethnic, economic group, etc. It is the rewriting of history to make people comfortable by ignoring facts - things that really happened - good or bad."[309]

"First and foremost it is punitive when it comes to issues of race, gender, sexuality and related topics. Transgressions must be punished no matter how long ago they occurred. It is also unforgiving… It is also primarily a left-wing ideology."[310]

Folk Catholicism – 1. an interesting blend of Roman Catholicism and animism; 2. Animism with the 'external trappings' or appearance of Roman Catholicism[311]

---

[309] pewresearch.org

[310] forbes.com/sites/evangerstmann/2021/03/22/what-is-cancel-culture/

[311] Filipino Spirit World by Rodney L. Henry, p.11

Political Correctness – Speech that is deemed unacceptable and offensive by liberals and liberal media.

Watershed moment – "A critical turning point in time where everything changes that will never be the same as before."

Wokeness or Wokeism – "Today's hottest religion. Joining it allows simple-minded people to pride themselves on believing they are more enlightened than, more compassionate than, and morally superior to, most of their fellow human beings."[312]

---

[312] urbandictionary.com/define.php?term=Wokeism

The proceeds from this book...

100% of the proceeds from sales of this book are dedicated to aiding both "children" of mine in fulfilling their God-appointed destinies:

Rhema Christian Training Center

Romulo National Hwy., San Juan de Mata,
Tarlac City 2300
PHILIPPINES
www.rhemaphilippines.org

Contact and "like" us on our Facebook pages:

@Rhema.Philippines
@RhemaFamilyChurchPhilippines
@ROLPreschool.Tarlac
@BettyCedergrenChildrensBook
@ComingOutAlive

 Donations for the ministry in the Philippines are welcome via PayPal using this QR code.

AGAPE Christian Centre

Grabenstrasse 1
CH-8952 Schlieren,
SWITZERLAND

Read Along with Me

– A collection of Short Stories and Poems for Children –

Betty V. Cedergren (1932-2019)

This collection of stories and poems have been gathered over many years, being tucked away in journals. Some stories are based on actual events, others from observing God's creation or influence in the daily lives of people. One story is from Liberia, West Africa, where Cedergren and her family lived and served as missionaries. Several stories and poems were written during their missionary days in the Philippines. 72 pages.

Betty V. Cedergren (1932-2019) with a Bachelor's Degree in elementary education, her teaching experience included more than 30 years of teaching K-2nd grade in the Minnesota public school system and in two different Christian schools. Betty and her husband, John (1929-2019), served as missionaries in Liberia, the Philippines, and Macau, China.

Available at: amazon.com

Type **"Betty Cedergren"** in the Amazon Search Bar

or directly from the publisher's website:

www.christianpublishers.org

Search "Children's Books" under the "CPH Bookstore" tab

Like us on Facebook 👍

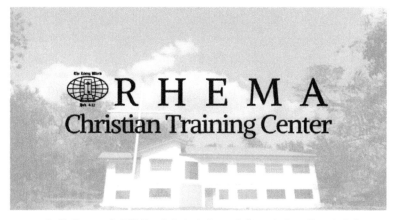

Full Gospel, Biblical & Ministerial Training for Adults

Rhema is a two-year Word of Faith based Ministerial Training Center located in Tarlac City, Philippines. Established in 1983, our objective is to train and equip men and women for full-time Christian missions, evangelism and local church ministry. Today, our graduates can be found in every corner of the Philippines, and indeed, around the world!

REQUIREMENTS:

1. Must be a minimum of 18 years old.
2. Must be born-again for at least one year and regularly attending a home church.
3. Must speak and understand English very well.
4. Must sense a genuine Call of God for Christian ministry and have serious desire and determination to prepare for that Calling.

HOW TO APPLY:

1. Fill up an application and be interviewed (in English) by our school administrator.
2. Provide the school with a Recommendation Letter from your home church pastor.
3. Bring two 1"x1" ID photos recently taken.
4. Fees apply.
CLASSES BEGINS IN JUNE EACH YEAR. In-person (in classroom) learning only.

CONTACT INFORMATION:

RHEMA Christian Training Center
Happy Valley, Romulo National Highway,
San Juan De Mata, Tarlac City 2300, PHILIPPINES
Phone Number: +63 906 491 6699
Email: rhematarlac@live.com
www.rhema.ph
Facebook RCTC Administrator: @Rhema.Christian.Tarlac

HOW TO SUPPORT
Rhema Christian Training Center
Philippines

BANK ACCOUNT DETAILS IN THE PHILIPPINES

BPI Tarlac City Hwy Branch
Macarthur Hwy, San Nicolas, Tarlac City 2300
Name on Account: Rhema Christian Center Philippines Inc
Account Nr.: 0533-4892-49
Branch Code: BR053
SWIFT Code: BOPIPHMM
Routing Number: 021000018

(If possible, please send a copy of your remittance slip or a short email detailing your name and the amount of your donation because the bank is not always able to report to us where or who the deposit came from. You will receive an email acknowledgement of your donation upon its crediting to the account. Please contact us at this email address regarding donations: ***rhema_ccpi@yahoo.com.ph***

TAX DEDUCTIBLE DONATIONS (U.S. only)

By Checks payable to:
Rhema Christian Center
P.O.Box 460, Golden, MS 38847 USA
Contact: Rev. Ed Garcia, 256-810-5771
(please write ***«for Rhema Philippines»*** on your check memo)

VIA PAYPAL

Donations for the ministry in the Philippines from anywhere in the world are welcome via PayPal using this QR code.

Printed in Great Britain
by Amazon